Andrew Cousins is a Barrister at DAC Beachcroft, a Door Tenant at 7 Harrington Street Chambers and a Visiting Law Lecturer at BPP Law School. He advises on a wide range of civil litigation matters. Andrew qualified as a Legal Executive in 2006, a Solicitor in 2011 and was called to the Bar by the Honourable Society of the Middle Temple in 2017. He was appointed to sit as an Assistant Coroner in 2018. Andrew has a background in personal injury, coronial and regulatory law. This is Andrew's second book, his first, 'A Practical Guide to the Compensation Recovery Unit and NHS Charges in England & Wales', was published in July 2020. Andrew has advised both Claimants and Defendants in relation to personal injury work and has given a number of training presentations on this area of law.

A Practical Guide to Surveillance Evidence in Personal Injury Claims in England and Wales

A Practical Guide to Surveillance Evidence in Personal Injury Claims in England and Wales

Andrew Cousins
Barrister, Middle Temple
LLM MRes

Law Brief Publishing

Published 2021 by Law Brief Publishing, an imprint of Law Brief Publishing Ltd
30 The Parks
Minehead
Somerset
TA24 8BT

www.lawbriefpublishing.com

Paperback: 978-1-913715-73-1

To my skydiving family,

for all your help and support

PREFACE

Surveillance evidence has existed in personal injury litigation for many years. Such evidence has been used to devastating effects to undermine the fabric of a claim, conversely some surveillance evidence has corroborated the validity of a claim advanced by the claimant. Surveillance evidence can be one of the most potent pieces of evidence disclosed in a case, at its most extreme, it can be so decisive that it can lead to criminal proceedings being brought against a litigant who has been exposed advancing a fraudulent claim for damages.

Even though this evidence has been a prominent feature in personal injury claims for a lengthy period of time, there is little legislation or statutory regulation governing the obtaining and deployment of this evidence. The law in this area has largely (but not exclusively) grown out of precedent.

It is a fact that in litigation some claims are brought by persons who are not always truthful about the effects that their accident has had upon their life, and surveillance evidence is a significant weapon in the arsenals of those seeking to counter such claims. Conversely, some defendants are suspicious of a great number of claims which are genuine. How the courts address the use of surveillance evidence has been a matter that has caused difficulties for many years. During this time, viewpoints have changed, the technology used to obtain surveillance footage has developed significantly, and the courts have had to frequently revisit the principles surrounding how this evidence is handled.

The purpose of this book is not to attack the credibility of any party in litigation, and it is not meant to promote or denigrate the actions of litigants who bring and defend claims. This book is written on the premise that surveillance evidence has been obtained by the defendant, this is because it is usually the case that surveillance evidence is obtained by defendants. In spite of this premise, this book is designed to be a neutral work with the aim to lay out the law in this field, to assist those who have to advise clients in this area.

In the same vein as my first book on the subject of the Compensation Recovery Unit, when I began writing this practical guide, I kept to the same goal, which was to provide a concise handbook to help practitioners address the issues facing them when considering the issue of surveillance evidence in personal injury claims.

There are areas of this book which can overlap with other chapters, but throughout the course of this work, I have tried to focus as much on the practical aspects of this area of law, so that the book can be as useful as is possible to those who have to grapple with these issues in practise. Whilst I have addressed the background to surveillance evidence, I have tried to steer away from a historical review of how the use of evidence has expanded in recent times, in order to focus on day-to-day practical issues.

Chapters six and seven address the issues of costs and future actions, these chapters are designed to give broad indications as to the issues in these areas of the law. The issues discussed in those chapters could be the subject of whole books in their own right, and as such a full analysis of the topics is beyond the remit of this text. The purpose of these chapters is to provide some indication as to how surveillance evidence can impact upon these aspects of litigation.

I do not by any means claim to be the preeminent expert in the field of surveillance law, there are many lawyers and academics with a detailed knowledge of the law and the issues in this area, which will easily surpass my own. The matters set out in this book address issues that frequently occur in dealing with the issue of surveillance evidence, and the framework around this area of law.

The book is directed towards practitioners of all levels who operate in the field of personal injury work, but will be most helpful for practitioners who are new to the field and have not had the opportunity to gather much experience in this area of litigation.

In closing, I would like to pass on my thanks to Tim Kevan and Garry Wright at Law Brief Publishing Ltd for all of their support throughout this project, and to David Boyle of Deans Court Chambers. David is a Barrister and respected author of a number of books. As I have continued my work as an author, his guidance has been extremely valued.

The law is believed to be accurate as at 13 May 2021.

Andrew Cousins
May 2021

LEGISLATION, STATUTORY INSTRUMENTS AND CASE LAW

Legislation

- Civil Evidence Act (1972)
- Contempt of Court Act (1981)
- Criminal Justice Act (2003)
- Criminal Justice and Courts Act (2015)
- Human Rights Act (1998)
- Investigatory Powers Act (2016)

Statutory Instruments

- The Civil Procedure (Amendment No 3) Rules 2020 (SI 2020/747)

Codes of Conduct

- Association of British Insurers Code of Ethics and Professional Standards
- Bar Standards Board Handbook
- Chartered Institute of Legal Executive's code of conduct
- Solicitors Regulation Authority code of conduct

Case Law

- Alan Mark Kearsely v Daniel Klarfield [2005] EWCA Civ 1510

- Aviva Insurance Ltd v Kovacic [2017] EWHC 2772 (QB)
- Amy Elizabeth Burrett v Mencap Limited [2014]
- Barings plc v Coopers & Lybrand [2001] PNLR 22
- Calderbank v Calderbank [1975] 3 All ER 333 (EWCA)
- Carol Walton v Joanne Kirk [2009] EWHC 703 (QB)
- Chadwick v Lewis & Aviva Insurance Ltd [2016] County Court sitting at Cardiff
- CIP Properties (AIPT) Ltd v Galliford Try Infrastructure Ltd [2015] EWHC 1345 (TCC)
- Dale v Banga & Others [2021] EWCA Civ 240
- Dass v Dass [2013] EWHC 2520 (QB)
- Denton v TH White Ltd [2014] EWCA Civ 906
- Faiz Siddiqui v The Chancellor, Masters and Scholars of The University of Oxford [2018] EWHC 536 (QB)
- Fairclough Homes Ltd v Summers [2012] UKSC 26
- Ford v GKR Construction Ltd and others [2000] 1 All ER 802
- Garcin and others v Amerindo Investment Advisors Ltd and others - [1991] 4 All ER 655
- George Eliot Hospital NHS Trust v Lesley Maria Elder [2019] EWHC 1813 (QB)
- Grant v Newport City Council [2018] EWHC 3813 Ch
- Grobbelaar v Sun Newspapers Ltd, The Times, 12 August 1999, CA
- Groveholt Ltd v Hughes [2010] EWCA Civ 538

- Hannon v Hillingdon Homes Limited [2013] EWHC 4553 (QB)
- Hibberd-Little v Carlton [2018] EWHC 1787 (QB)
- Hicks v Rostas and Motor Insurance Bureau High Court (QB) His Honour Judge Reddihough 17 March 2017
- Howlett v Davies [2017] EWHC Civ 1696
- Ivey v Genting Casinos (UK) Ltd [2017] UKSC 67
- Jason Tully v (1) Exterion Media (UK) Ltd (In Liquidation) (2) London Underground Ltd [2020] EWHC 1119 (QB)
- Jayne Ellen Evans v Royal Wolverhampton Hospitals NHS Foundation Trust [2014] EWHC 3185 (QB)
- Jones v University of Warwick [2003] EWCA Civ 151
- Karapetianas v Kent and Sussex Loft Conversions Ltd [2017] EWHC 859 (QB)
- Katrina Draper v Nottingham City Council [2017] 11 WLUK 644
- Kennedy v Cordia Services (LLP) [2016] UKSC 6
- Khan (Avrangzeb) v Armaguard Ltd. [1994] 1 W.L.R. 1204 (CA)
- Kilbey v Arien Contractors Ltd [2019] Lexis Citation 470
- Kuruma v Queen, The [1955] A.C. 197, [1955] 1 WLUK 425
- Ladd v Marshall [1954] 3 All ER 745
- London Organising Committee of the Olympic and Paralympic Games v Sinfield [2018] EWHC 51 (QB)
- Lord Advocate v Blantyre (1879) 4 App. Cas 770:

- Lorna Catherine Hayden v Maidstone & Tunbridge Wells NHS Trust [2016] EWHC 1121 (QB)
- Lumb v Hampsey (2011) EWHC 2808 (QB)
- Marcus v Medway Primary Care Trust [2011] EWCA Civ 750
- Marlene Samson v Mohammed Ali [2012] EWHC 4146 (QB)
- Martin Raymond Owens v Mark Noble [2010] EWCA Civ 224
- Masquerade Music Ltd & Ors v Mr Bruce Springsteen EWCA Civ 563
- McNally v RG Manufacturing Ltd [1999] 12 WLUK 105
- Michael Gosling v (1) Hailo & (2) Screwfix Direct [2014] Lexis Citation 316
- Miley v Friends Life Ltd [2017] EWHC 2415 (QB)
- Morgan v UPS [2008] EWCA Civ 1476
- Mr Mohamed Rizan & Mr Mohamed Rilshad v (1) Barry Hayes (2) Allianz Insurance Plc [2016] EWCA Civ 4810
- O'Leary v Tunnelcraft Ltd [2009] EWHC 3438 (QB)
- Otkritie v International Investment Management Ltd v Gersamia and another [2015] EWHC 821 (Comm)
- Patel v Arriva Midlands Ltd and another [2019] EWHC 1216 (QB)
- Pendragon Motor Company Ltd t/a Stratstone (Wilmslow) Ltd v Mr A K Ridge [2001] UKEAT 962_00_0511
- Purser (Gemma) v Hibbs (Robert) & Anr judgment [2015] EWHC 1792 (QB)

- Quah v Goldman Sachs International [2015] EWHC 759 (Comm)
- R v Bonython (1984) 38 SASR 45
- R v Khan (Sultan) [1997] A.C. 558, [1996] 7 WLUK 26
- Russell Adrian Knibbs v (1) Heart of England NHS Foundation Trust (2) Dr G Koshy (3) Dr P Mehta [2017] Lexis Citation 311
- Sally Rall v Ross Hume [2001] EWCA Civ 146
- Sebastian James Wilcox v King's College Hospital NHS Foundation Trust [2020] EWHC 2555 (QB)
- Singh and others v Habib and another [2011] EWCA Civ 599
- South Wales Fire and Rescue Service v Smith [2011] EWHC 1740 (Admin)
- Spencer Smith v Ashwell Maintenance Ltd [2019] 1 WLUK 541
- SPR North Ltd v Swiss Post International (UK) Ltd [2019] EWHC 2004 (Ch)
- Stewart v Kelly [2016] EWHC 3263 (QB)
- Sudhirkumar Patel v (1) Arriva Midlands Ltd (2) Zurich Insurance PLC [2019] EWHC 1216 (QB)
- Tavenor Joe Douglas (A Protected Party By his Litigation Friend William Robertson) v Matthew James O'Neill [2011] EWHC 601 (QB)
- Tess Garraway v Holland & Barrett Ltd [2020] 3 WLUK 582
- Uttley v Uttley [2001] Lexis Citation 1948
- Vernon v Bosley [1994] P.I.Q.R.337

- Victoria Admans v Two Saints Ltd [2016] 6 WLUK 611
- Vukota-Bojic v Switzerland [2016] ECHR 1006/07
- Watson v Ministry of Defence [2016] EWHC 3163 (QB)
- Widlake v BAA Ltd [2009] EWCA Civ 1256
- Wright v Satellite Information [2018] EWHC 812 (QB)
- Yvonne Hazel Painting v University of Oxford [2005] EWCA Civ 161

CONTENTS

CHAPTER ONE

THE ADMISSIBILITY OF SURVEILLANCE EVIDENCE

For practitioners who must advise clients on cases involving surveillance evidence, there can be many issues to consider. Questions over how to obtain surveillance evidence, when to deploy it and its effect on the case are some of the most significant practical points that can be considered in a claim. Before these issues are considered, there are important points that need to be contemplated concerning the rules of evidence and whether the courts will allow such evidence to be admitted and relied upon in the litigation process.

As will be discussed in subsequent chapters, surveillance evidence is often disclosed after much of the evidence in a claim has been exchanged. It is evidence that needs to be kept secret for some time in order that the claimant is not made aware of the fact that they are being observed, and it is evidence that needs to be served as a surprise to the claimant. This is because the whole purpose of such evidence is that it is designed to capture the claimant undertaking activities that undermine the fabric of the claim. For these reasons, surveillance evidence is case managed in a different manner by the courts.

Whilst the above practical considerations are important for litigants, they do not affect the fundamental principle that surveillance footage, like anything else a litigant discloses, serves, or relies upon in a case is evidence, and just like all evidence it is subject to evidential rules. This chapter looks at the evidential rules, how surveillance evidence relates to those evidential principles, its admissibility, relevance, weight, and how the civil procedure rules ('CPR') address surveillance evidence.

Admissibility

The admissibility of evidence and the relevance of evidence are two different concepts that overlap in some regard. Not all evidence that is relevant is admissible, as we will see in chapter two, evidence may be relevant, but it may be inadmissible for example, on the grounds of public policy or because it has been obtained through unlawful means. The courts have a variety of powers to control evidence, these powers do not derive only from the court's case management powers under CPR 3, but through further sections of the CPR and additionally through the common law. In ***Kuruma v The Queen [1955] A.C. 197, [1955] 1 WLUK 425***, Lord Goddard CJ held that:

> ***the test to be applied in considering whether evidence is admissible is whether it is relevant to the matters in issue. If it is, it is admissible and the court is not concerned with how the evidence was obtained. While this proposition may not have been stated in so many words in any English case there are decisions which support it, and in their Lordships' opinion it is plainly right in principle. However, the court retains a wide discretion to exclude evidence.***

As can be seen, the court, at that time considered that evidence would be admissible regardless of how it is obtained. This is an example of how the law has developed over time, now the court's discretion to exclude evidence can extend to considering the manner in which the evidence was obtained. The CPR has given the court a range of powers to address the admissibility of evidence. The court has an inherent power under the court's case management powers to exclude an issue from consideration and ***CPR 3.1(2)(k)*** provides:

> ***(2) Except where these Rules provide otherwise, the court may –***
>
> > ***(k) exclude an issue from consideration***

In addition to this the court has a power under ***CPR 32.1*** to control the evidence in a case, the rule provides:

> ***(1) The court may control the evidence by giving directions as to –***
>
> > ***(a) the issues on which it requires evidence;***

> ***(b) the nature of the evidence which it requires to decide those issues; and***
>
> ***(c) the way in which the evidence is to be placed before the court.***

> ***(2) The court may use its power under this rule to exclude evidence that would otherwise be admissible.***

If a court is to exercise its powers under this rule to exclude evidence, then, as set out in ***Grobbelaar v Sun Newspapers Ltd, The Times, 12 August 1999 CA***, such a step must be taken with the overriding objective in mind and with a view to dealing with cases justly.

Therefore, even if a party obtains surveillance evidence that they disclose and is of relevance to the case, it can be excluded by the court under its provision to control evidence. When considering the admissibility of relevant evidence, and whether or not it should be excluded, the court has to consider the weight of the evidence, this is sometimes referred to as the probative value of the evidence. The less probative value the evidence has to the issues in the case, the more likely a court would be to exercise its powers to exclude the evidence. There is therefore some overlap between the evidential rules of admissibility and relevance.

Relevance

In order to determine if the surveillance evidence is relevant to the issues in the case, the footage must be carefully reviewed, and cross referenced to the statements of case. How relevant the footage will be is a factual issue that will vary from case to case, for example surveillance footage that shows a claimant able to walk a great distance unaided will be of little assistance if the claimant's witness statement alleges that he can mobilise without difficulty. Conversely surveillance evidence showing the claimant driving a vehicle for work will be of great assistance if the claimant's claim is founded on the premise that the accident has left them physically incapable of work and driving.

It is only through a close scrutiny of the claimant's evidence and statements of case that the relevance of the surveillance evidence can be determined. Relevance cannot be a static concept, what will be relevant to one case and one set of facts will of course not relate to a different claim. For this reason, the parties and the courts have to identify the facts in issue in the claim and how the surveillance evidence assists the court with determining those facts. As set out in ***Vernon v Bosley [1994] P.I.Q.R.337***, by Hoffman LJ:

> ***The degree of relevance needed for admissibility is not some fixed point on a scale, but will vary according to the nature of the evidence and in particular the inconvenience, expense, delay or oppression which would attend its reception.***

Surveillance evidence that does not address the issues in the case (or worse is footage taken of the wrong person), will not be of assistance to the court and may be excluded. This is highlighted by the case of ***Sebastian James Wilcox v King's College Hospital NHS Foundation Trust [2020] EWHC 2555 (QB)***, where Lambert J disallowed the defendant permission to rely upon surveillance evidence. The claimant had alleged that because of a delay in diagnosis of cauda equina, he had limited mobility and needed daily living and care assistance. The defendant sought permission to rely upon surveillance footage that, it alleged addressed the claimant's position on functional capabilities. At first instance and on appeal, the court considered that the surveillance footage did not highlight any significant inconsistencies in the claimant's case. The evidence was disallowed on the grounds that it was not relevant to the case advanced by the claimant.

This is an example of how the courts can, and do, exercise their powers to disallow evidence. Even though the evidence was properly obtained, it was excluded as it did not relate to the issues in the case. It also serves to highlight that the analysis of the relevancy of surveillance evidence has to be conducted by reference to the pleaded case advanced by the claimant, and compared with the surveillance footage. Litigants may therefore lose the ability to rely upon surveillance footage should the court exercise its case management powers to exclude the matter from consideration.

Weight

In personal injury litigation there are not often many cases in which a 'silver bullet' of evidence proves or destroys a case, parties frequently accumulate a variety of evidence in order to build a picture to support their pleaded position. Surveillance evidence can sometimes be the exception to this rule and at times the 'silver bullet' of evidence. In the same way that the relevance of evidence cannot be determined by a static refence, neither can the weight of evidence. As set out by Lord Blackburn in ***Lord Advocate v Blantyre (1879) 4 App. Cas 770***:

> ***The weight of evidence depends on rules of common sense.***

If the defendant is permitted to rely upon the surveillance evidence, then the weight that is to be attached to the evidence is a matter for the trial judge having considered the totality of the evidence, and having heard the lay witness and expert evidence and considered the documents in relation to the issues in the case. Key considerations for the court are who bears the burden of proof, are there any risks associated with putting weight on the surveillance evidence and if so, what are they. The court must consider whether the evidence can be thoroughly tested or, is it incomplete and incapable of the same level of interrogation as the remaining evidence in the case.

The best evidence rule

As touched upon above, an issue for many courts is what weight can be placed upon the surveillance evidence. If the evidence cannot be interrogated to the same level as other evidence in the case, then it may cause the court to question what weight it can place upon the evidence. It is a fact of litigation that not all evidence is perfect. Some evidence can be incomplete, for example with surveillance footage the person under surveillance is not always in camera shot and can disappear for lengths of time, can the footage be said to be complete if the claimant cannot always be seen? How this affects what weight the court can place upon the footage must be determined by the quality of the footage compared to the claimant's statements of case.

The best evidence rule has developed over a considerable amount of time in the course of legal history. As set out in ***Phipson on Evidence 19th Ed. 7-40***:

> ***In the present day, then, it is not true that the best evidence must, or even may, always be given, though its non-production may be a matter for comment, or affect the weight of that which is produced. All admissible evidence is generally equally accepted.***

The court of appeal examined the best evidence rule in the case of *Masquerade Music Ltd & Ors v Mr Bruce Springsteen [2001] EWCA Civ 563*, wherein Parker LJ held that:

> ***a party to whom a document is available will by reason of that very fact be unable to account to the satisfaction of the court for his non-production of it when inviting the court to admit secondary evidence of its contents, with the practical consequence that the court will attach no weight to the secondary evidence.***

And:

> ***In my judgment, the time has now come when it can be said with confidence that the best evidence rule, long on its deathbed, has finally expired. In every case where a party seeks to adduce secondary evidence of the contents of a document, it is a matter for the court to decide, in the light of all the circumstances of the case, what (if any) weight to attach to that evidence. Where the party seeking to adduce the secondary evidence could readily produce the document, it may be expected that (absent some special circumstances) the court will decline to admit the secondary evidence on the ground that it is worthless. At the other extreme, where the party seeking to adduce the secondary evidence genuinely cannot produce the document, it may be expected that (absent some special circumstances) the court will admit the secondary evidence and attach such weight to it as it considers appropriate in all the circumstances. In cases falling between those two extremes, it is for the court to make a judgment as to whether in all the circumstances any weight***

> ***should be attached to the secondary evidence. Thus, the 'admissibility' of secondary evidence of the contents of documents is, in my judgment, entirely dependent upon whether or not any weight is to be attached to that evidence. And whether or not any weight is to be attached to such secondary evidence is a matter for the court to decide, taking into account all the circumstances of the particular case.***

Imperfect evidence is a situation that parties, and the courts have to face in litigation. Simply because a full and complete video log of surveillance footage is not always available in every case does not automatically mean that all of the surveillance evidence is to be excluded or cannot be relied upon. As set out by Parker LJ, the court may exclude the evidence if no special circumstance can be provided as to why the complete evidence is not available. It is for the court to consider the particular circumstances of each case and decide whether any weight can be placed on the imperfect evidence.

Civil Procedure Rules

When the CPR was introduced, the question of how surveillance evidence would be handled within the framework of those rules had to be addressed. The CPR promotes a 'cards on the table' approach to litigation, parties should make disclosure of evidence at an early stage in order to narrow the issues in a claim. During litigation, the court should make directions to give a structure as to when documentary evidence, expert evidence and witness evidence was to be disclosed. The parties to litigation are supposed to be allowed to know the case that is being advanced so that they can prepare accordingly, narrow issues to avoid complications and encourage settlement.

Whilst the introduction of the CPR streamlined the litigation process, it inevitably led to a number of questions as to how to handle the disclosure of evidence, and in particular surveillance evidence. The surprise disclosure of, potentially, significantly important new evidence did not sit easily within the structured approach to the litigation process. This prompted the question as to where in such a system surveillance evidence should feature, and what notice a litigant who had obtained such evidence needed to give in order to comply with the provisions of the

CPR. The issues in relation to the timing of disclosure of surveillance evidence are discussed in more detail in chapter three.

In considering how the CPR addresses the issue of surveillance evidence, the first question that had to be asked, and it may seem odd to ask the question, was what is a 'document'. ***CPR 31.4*** provides:

> ***In this Part –***
>
> ***'document' means anything in which information of any description is recorded;***

For the purposes of disclosure, surveillance footage is a recording of information and is therefore a document within the extended meaning contained in CPR 31.4, as established in ***Garcin and others v Amerindo Investment Advisors Ltd and others [1991] 4 All ER 655***. The next issue to consider is why that document has been brought into existence. Clearly such evidence did not exist prior to the claim being instigated. Surveillance evidence is a document brought into existence for the purposes of the litigation and is therefore privileged. In respect of the standard list of documents, surveillance evidence is not disclosable in part 1 of the list of documents, and the party obtaining the footage will seek to claim privilege over the evidence.

When a party is preparing its list of documents, a party can claim privilege over a document and seek not to disclose the same at the point of disclosure. This is important in relation to surveillance evidence, as the directions concerning disclosure usually take place early in the litigation process, and a party who has obtained surveillance evidence will wish to keep it secret until such time as the claimant has confirmed their case.

Privileged evidence is not disclosable in the first part of the list of documents which parties exchange in order to disclose the documents that they hold. A litigant who proposes to use surveillance evidence to attack another party's case will waive privilege when they disclose the evidence, and it will therefore be subject to the rules as to disclosure and inspection of documents contained in CPR 31.

Once privilege is waived and the surveillance evidence disclosed, the disclosing party will have waived privilege over the whole of the footage and must therefore disclose the entirety of the footage, they cannot rely upon chosen extracts. Whilst the party placed under surveillance may only be visible in some short sections of the footage, the disclosing party has to be candid about the full footage that has been obtained, this is consistent with the cards on the table approach to litigation. The party placed under surveillance is entitled to see if any of the footage obtained shows evidence that is supportive of their case. Once privilege is waived in part of the document, the whole document must be disclosed. This will mean that not only is the full footage disclosable, but that the video logs kept by the surveillance agents who obtained the footage are disclosable as well.

When the surveillance footage is disclosed, the claimant is deemed to admit the authenticity of the footage, unless a challenge is raised to the evidence. If the claimant wishes to challenge the authenticity of the footage, then it is incumbent upon them to serve notice that they wish it to be proved at trial. Such note is required pursuant to ***CPR 32.19*** which provides:

> ***(1) A party shall be deemed to admit the authenticity of a document disclosed to him under Part 31 (disclosure and inspection of documents) unless he serves notice that he wishes the document to be proved at trial.***
>
> ***(2) A notice to prove a document must be served –***
>
> > ***(a) by the latest date for serving witness statements; or***
> >
> > ***(b) within 7 days of disclosure of the document, whichever is later.***

As such a claimant who wishes to challenge the authenticity of the surveillance footage only has a short period of time to do so pursuant to ***CPR 32.19(2)(b)***. If a notice to prove a document is served, then the defendant must serve a witness statement by the surveillance operative who took the film in order to prove its authenticity.

The point as to what standing video surveillance footage has, was considered by the court of appeal in the case of ***Sally Rall v Ross Hume [2001] EWCA Civ 146.*** The court held that a video film was a document within the meaning of ***CPR 31.4.*** It is therefore subject to the rules as to disclosure contained in CPR 31.

The showing of a video requires facilities to be made available by the court to enable footage to be viewed and it extends the time for the trial. There is a duty upon the party seeking to rely upon the video to help the court to further the overriding objective, and this means that the matter should be raised at the first practicable opportunity. The starting point of any application to rely upon video evidence, where the evidence according to the defendant undermines the case of the claimant, is that it must be in the overall interest of justice to allow the claimant and the claimant's medical experts, to be cross-examined by the defendant. As will be examined in later chapters, this does not mean that the defendant can conduct a trial by ambush and safeguards must be put into place to ensure that the disclosure of surveillance evidence does not derail the trial timetable.

CHAPTER TWO

OBTAINING SURVEILLANCE EVIDENCE

When a party decides to obtain surveillance evidence there are considerations as to how, when and where such evidence is obtained and who should be instructed to obtain it. Some of these considerations are tactical issues that a party must take depending upon the particular circumstances of each case. There are however various common threads and legal principles that can be seen running through these considerations.

How and when surveillance evidence can be obtained

The party wishing to obtain the evidence will instruct a surveillance agent or company to obtain video footage of the litigant. Therefore, the actual obtaining of the footage is somewhat out of the hands of the instructing party as it is obtained by the surveillance agents. It is often they who exercise their judgement as to when they may be able to locate the litigant and obtain video footage of them. A letter of instruction setting out the claimant's details, whereabouts, position, and information is sent to the surveillance agent in order that they may ascertain how best to obtain relevant footage of the claimant.

As set out in the preface, this book is a neutral work and does not take a side in relation to the rights and wrongs of the actions of litigants in a particular case. For parties obtaining surveillance evidence though, there are often ethical considerations, as they may wish to ensure that they do not taint their business by having surveillance evidence obtained through improper methodology. This issue is discussed in more detail below, but at the outset, the careful selection of which surveillance agent is instructed to obtain the footage can be an important consideration for the instructing litigant.

It is commonplace to see footage which shows a litigant under surveillance on more than one occasion. If footage is taken over a short period, or only shows a limited amount of time where the litigant is seen on camera, then the disclosing party leaves themselves open to a response that the claimant has 'good and bad days', and the footage simply saw them on a 'bad day', this is discussed in more detail in chapter four. In such circumstances, the weight of the evidence is reduced, and the court may feel that it cannot place much reliance upon it. To have the best effect, the defendant will wish to submit evidence to the court displaying a pattern of behaviour by the claimant that is inconsistent with their statements of case and expert medical evidence.

A common time for a litigant to be placed under surveillance is when they are attending a medico legal examination arranged by the party obtaining the footage. This is a favourite time to obtain surveillance evidence because it is known where the litigant will be and roughly what route they will be taking to reach the examination, making it easier to locate and film them. The stages at which footage is obtained though are often agreed between the instructing litigant and the surveillance agent so that the remit, and most importantly the costs of the footage, can be clearly understood.

A certain amount of control over the manner in which the surveillance evidence is obtained is exercised by the company obtaining the footage. The particular factors of the case may inform how best to obtain the footage, is following the claimant's everyday movements the most appropriate option? Is a static camera fixed outside of the claimant's property a better method? Having a surveillance agent following the claimant may be more costly, but will likely obtain more varied footage of the claimant's functional abilities. It may also increase the chances of the claimant becoming aware that they have been placed under surveillance. A static camera fixed on one point may have the advantage of saving costs, but will capture more limited footage of the claimant. The use of a static camera may be of advantage where, for example, the claimant contends that they are unable to leave the house, and fixed cameras can record instances of the claimant acting contrary to such a statement. These are matters which need to be considered based upon the facts of the claim being advanced, and agreed with the surveillance company engaged in obtaining the footage.

Human rights implications

Persons who are placed under surveillance may sometimes consider the collection of the video footage to be intrusive and an invasion of their privacy. From their perspective they have, without their knowledge or consent, been covertly filmed, they may not have been aware that such evidence is obtained in the litigation process or is allowed to be used. The existence of such footage can come as a significant shock to them, even before the content of the video is viewed, and they may feel very angry that they have been subjected to these tactics.

It cannot be correct that a party obtaining such footage can simply obtain video evidence of a litigant at any time, in any location and through any means physically available to them. As we saw in chapter one, the court has the power to control evidence in a case through its powers under the CPR, but this is not the only safeguard that exists. A litigant does not surrender all rights to respect for their home and private and family life simply because they bring a claim for damages. **The Human Rights Act (1998)** ('the human rights act') affords various protections in this regard.

With the implementation of the Human Rights Act, the courts have had to consider how the Act has impacted upon the right to obtain surveillance evidence, and the right to not be placed under surveillance when a person has a reasonable expectation that they are conducting their private business. The point to be considered is the manner in which surveillance evidence has been collected because this is relevant to its admissibility.

The courts have recognised the need for safeguards in this area, and in the case of ***Hannon v Hillingdon Homes Limited [2013] EWHC 4553 (QB)***, the high court held that:

> ***I should add that a further reason for particular concern about surveillance evidence is that without good justification and without a very careful following of appropriate safeguards, filming a private individual is, or is certainly potentially, a very significant breach of that claimant's rights under the Human Rights Act as being a very serious invasion of that person's private and family life.***

There are two Articles to the Human Rights Act that are relevant to this topic, and they are **Article 6** and **Article 8**. **Article 6** provides:

> ***In the determination of his civil rights and obligations or of any criminal charge against him, everyone is entitled to a fair and public hearing within a reasonable time by an independent and impartial tribunal established by law.***

Article 8 provides:

> ***Everyone has the right to respect for his private and family life, his home and his correspondence.***
>
> ***There shall be no interference by a public authority with the exercise of this right except such as is in accordance with the law and is necessary in a democratic society in the interests of national security, public safety or the economic well-being of the country, for the prevention of disorder or crime, for the protection of health or morals, or for the protection of the rights and freedoms of others.***

Whilst the Human Rights Act does not confer a direct duty on claimants, most defendants, insurers, or surveillance agents, it does impose a duty on the courts. The courts, as a public authority, must ensure respect for the provisions, set out at Articles 6 and 8 of the Human Rights Act.

When considering these Articles, parties obtaining surveillance footage at first advanced the position that the right to a fair trial under Article 6 would be infringed if the video footage were to be excluded from the case. This could potentially lead to a false claim not being revealed if the court did not consider the footage, and would be an injustice.

On behalf of parties placed under surveillance, the position has been taken that, in order to carry out their duty to protect the Article 8 right, the courts should prevent defendants from relying on evidence that was obtained in breach of the claimant's right to privacy. If the evidence had been obtained by unlawful means, it has been argued that this was all the more reason to uphold the Article 8 right and exclude the surveillance evidence.

The courts have had to consider these two competing interests. The issue can be distilled to asking this: where does the balance lie between the public interest in discovering the truth in a case, and the public interest in ensuring that the courts do not permit the improperly obtained evidence to be deployed?

Improperly obtained evidence

Just as it is a fact of litigation that not all claims are presented honestly, there are instances where not all surveillance evidence has been obtained, handled, and stored, properly and ethically. A discussion as to the exact circumstances of improperly obtained surveillance evidence is beyond the scope of this text, and in any event no comprehensive list can be finalised. Some examples of improperly obtained evidence have included occasions where claimants have been befriended by surveillance agents and then, on reliance of that false friendship placed under surveillance. There have been instances where claimants have been tricked into allowing evidence to be recorded from within their own homes, where one might have a reasonable expectation of privacy.

A difficulty has arisen where the footage, though obtained through improper means, has shown relevant evidence that undermines the claim and/or strikes at the heart of issues in the statements of case. The courts have had to determine how to address such evidence and balance the relevance of the evidence as against the improper methods by which it has been obtained.

Two early decisions on these points can be seen in the case of ***McNally v RG Manufacturing Ltd [1999] 12 WLUK 105***, and in ***R. v Khan (Sultan) [1997] A.C. 558, [1996] 7 WLUK 26***. In ***McNally***, the defendant had denied that the claimant had been injured, and submitted surveillance evidence in support of their position. The evidence had been obtained by surveillance agents who had entered the claimant's house purporting to be market researchers, in addition they had filmed the claimant in the street. The evidence revealed that the claimant was considerably less disabled than he claimed.

In giving judgment, HHJ Harris QC sitting in the county court at Northampton held that, despite the questionable methods of obtaining the video evidence, it was admissible given that the evidence was relevant. The misleading of a dishonest claimant might be both excusable and necessary to prevent him from succeeding with an exaggerated claim.

In ***Khan*** the police had obtained the evidence against the defendant by fixing a covert listening device at an apartment visited by the defendant, and by recording his conversations there. The court held that there was no right of privacy which is sufficient to justify the exclusion of evidence which had been obtained by electronic bugging of a private house. The court found that as a matter of English law, evidence which is obtained improperly or even unlawfully remains admissible, subject to the power of the trial judge to exclude it in the exercise of his common law discretion. It is questionable whether such a position of 'the ends justify the means' would still be permissible in light of the developments in jurisprudence, and further demonstrates the changing attitudes of the courts towards surveillance evidence over the years that the case law has developed.

There was a break in time before an appellate authority was available. When faced with this issue, the court reached the conclusion that even in cases where the party in possession of the evidence must have acted unlawfully in order to obtain it, there is a balance between the competing public interests outlined above. The court of appeal addressed the position in the case of ***Jones v University of Warwick [2003] EWCA Civ 151.***

In this case, the claimant had made a claim for damages following an accident at work. Liability had been admitted and the claimant sought damages in excess of £135,000, on the basis that the injury to her right wrist was causing ongoing disability. The defendant instructed a private investigator who attended the claimant's home on two occasions under the guise of being a market researcher. During these visits, the claimant was covertly filmed using her right hand in a manner which appeared inconsistent with her pleaded claim. The defendant's medical experts considered that the claimant was able to use her hand without difficulty, although this was not agreed by the claimant's medical experts.

The defendant applied for permission to rely upon the surveillance evidence. In response, the claimant contended that the evidence should be excluded because of the private investigator's trespass, the infringement of the claimant's Article 8 right and invasion of her privacy.

The court of appeal allowed the defendant to rely upon the evidence, but considered that there was no satisfactory way by which the conflicting public policies could be reconciled. The exclusion of relevant video evidence would create an artificial and undesirable situation. To mark its disapproval of the defendant's conduct however, the court was entitled to penalise the defendant in costs. Clearly the issue posed the court of appeal a significant difficulty, the court not only acknowledged that there was no satisfactory way reconcile the public policy arguments, but went further, Lord Woolf CJ stated:

> ***We do not pretend that this is a perfect reconciliation of the conflicting public interests. It is not; but at least the solution does not ignore the insurers' conduct.***

Interestingly the court approached the matter from the perspective of the management of the litigation and exercise of discretion and stated:

> ***Proactive management of civil proceedings, which is at the heart of the CPR, is not only concerned with an individual piece of litigation which is before the Court, it is also concerned with litigation as a whole. So the fact that in this case the defendant's insurers, as was accepted by Mr Owen, have been responsible for the trespass involved in entering the claimant's house and infringing her privacy contrary to Article 8(1) is a relevant circumstance for the court to weigh in the balance when coming to a decision as to how it should properly exercise its discretion in making orders as to the management of the proceedings.***

It cannot always be said that evidence obtained improperly will always be permitted by the court. In ***Sally Rall v Ross Hume [2001] EWCA Civ 146***, the court exercised its powers to exclude some of the surveillance evidence. The claimant had brought a claim for damages to her neck, shoulder, lower back and psychological injuries. The pleaded claim made representations that the claimant suffered significant limitations on activities, including driving and caring for her children. In response, the defendants undertook surveillance operations in February and August 2000, the evidence was disclosed to the claimant in June and October 2000. The footage showed the claimant making journeys by car and engaged in child-care activities seemingly without difficulty.

On 6 November 2000 the matter was listed for disposal and this hearing was due to take place on 22 January 2001. On 13 December, the defendant's application to rely on the video evidence was refused. Following an unsuccessful appeal, the matter reached the court of appeal. The court took as its starting position the following:

> ***In principle, as it seems to me, the starting point on any application of this kind must be that, where video evidence is available which, according to the defendant, undermines the case of the claimant to an extent that would substantially reduce the award of damages to which she is entitled, it will usually be in the overall interests of justice to require that the defendant should be permitted to cross-examine the Plaintiff and her medical advisors upon it, so long as this does not amount to trial by ambush.***

The issue of whether the evidence amounts to an ambush, and the timing of disclosure will be considered in chapter three, but in ***Rall***, footage had been obtained from within the claimant's home and taken whilst visiting a nursery. Some of this evidence was held to be improperly obtained and was excluded by the court exercising its case management powers. Litigants therefore have to be very clear as to how the evidence was obtained and whether any subterfuge was used in the manner of the recording.

Some examples of instances where surveillance evidence which has not been allowed to be used by the defendant because of the means by which such evidence has been obtained, have included occasions where agents have entered the claimant's property and filmed through a claimant's windows, tipped over his dustbin in order to film the claimant picking up rubbish from his path, entered into the claimant's home by pretending to be a door to door sales person or befriending the claimant and getting invited into his house. Reliance upon such footage can leave litigants open to arguments that the court should not only exclude such evidence, but should revisit the costs of the same upon the party seeking to rely upon the footage.

Public authorities

The matters discussed above have all related to surveillance evidence obtained by insurance companies or private defendants. The issue of how surveillance evidence is obtained by a public authority is different.

In ***Vukota-Bojic v Switzerland [2016] ECHR 1006/07***, the European Court of Human Rights held that where surveillance has been carried out secretly, by a public authority, that this constituted a breach of Article 8. The two key factors in the case were firstly that Article 8 applied because the defendant was acting on behalf of the state. Secondly, that the surveillance carried out had systematically and intentionally watched the claimant and that they had stored, selected, and used the material beyond legitimate and foreseeable purposes. Therefore, it amounted to a breach of Article 8. The court stated that:

> ***where surveillance has been carried out secretly, by a public authority, that this constituted a breach of ECHR, art 8—'right to respect for private life and family life'. The two key principles were firstly that art 8 applied because the defendant was acting on behalf of the state (in many personal injury cases, investigations are almost exclusively carried out by private entities such as insurance companies and therefore art 8 is not applicable). Secondly, that the surveillance carried out had systematically and intentionally watched the claimant and that they had stored, selected and used the material beyond legitimate and foreseeable purposes. Therefore it amounted to a breach of ECHR, art 8(1).***

The ***Investigatory Powers Act (2016)*** impacts upon how public authorities may obtain surveillance evidence. Public authorities wishing to conduct covert surveillance have to ensure that operations are authorised by a 'senior authorising officer'. Authorisation must be deemed necessary on one or more of the specified grounds, and will be withheld unless the surveillance is proportionate to what is sought to be achieved by carrying it out.

Safeguards exist in the form that, in order to obtain authorisation for surveillance to be conducted, an application is required which must set out in detail the nature of the intended surveillance, details of potential intrusion to the claimant, and why the intrusion is justified. The application must establish reasons why the surveillance is considered proportionate to what its intended objectives are.

An application may be refused if a less intrusive method of obtaining the evidence is available, in this situation that method must be used and the risk of obtaining private information about other people must be assessed. The aim of the provisions is to ensure that the risk of the state breaching the Human Rights Act articles is minimised and that the unnecessary intrusion to privacy of those not intended to be part of investigation is reduced to its lowest level.

Future Issues

There is clearly some degree of disparity in the regulatory framework surrounding how private companies may obtain surveillance evidence and how public authorities may do so, the provisions examined above in relation to applications being made by public authorities to justify the obtaining of such evidence do not apply to private insurance companies. This section is not intended to advocate either for or against a regulatory framework in this area, but to outline some of the issues. At present there has been some criticism of how lax the regulation is surrounding private investigation. Following ***Jones v Warwick University*** commentators have noted the improper methodology by which evidence has been gathered, and this has led to calls for regulation in this area of law.

It has been suggested that the best long-term solution would be to have a regulatory scheme for private investigators requiring that they be licenced. Alongside a regulatory scheme, solicitors could ensure that only appropriate and proportionate measures are used to obtain surveillance footage. This would require an amendment to the Solicitors Code of Conduct to ensure that solicitors maintain a policy on the commissioning of surveillance operations. Furthermore, that court permission must be obtained prior to the surveillance evidence being obtained. Such an application would have to satisfy a court that the obtaining of the evidence would be done ethically, that it would be proportionate, relevant and would not disrupt the court timetable.

If a requirement was introduced to ensure that an application had to be made before surveillance evidence was obtained, then this would need to be made without notice initially, to do otherwise would simply alert the claimant to the presence of such tactics. Once the footage has been obtained, an application hearing would take place at which the claimant would be given an opportunity to make representations about whether or not the footage should be admitted.

At present, the above issues are only some of the general ideas that have been discussed as to the possible developments of regulation in this area. It has been argued that this is an area of law which, because of technological advancement and the widening use of surveillance evidence, that regulation is long overdue. As such this is an area where they may be developments in respect of regulation in the future.

Proving Admissible Evidence

Obtaining surveillance evidence is one thing, but how can the disclosing party actually ensure that the evidence can then be relied upon in the litigation? If the evidence is admitted by the court, then the disclosing party must prove the evidence.

As we saw above in ***Jones v University of Warwick***, the surveillance evidence, and its effect on the claimant's pleaded claim may not be agreed, often it is contested. The party disclosing the evidence must therefore address how the footage can be proved in evidence before the court. In ***Rall v Hume***, Potter LJ held:

> ***If the claimant does not challenge the authenticity of the film, however, it is in the absence of any ruling by the Court to the contrary, available to the defendant for the purposes of cross-examining the claimant and/or the claimant's expert medical witnesses at Court.***

The starting point is therefore, does the claimant challenge the authenticity of the footage? The claimant should note the principles in ***CPR 32.19,*** which were also examined in chapter one, which requires notice to be given of such a challenge within a specified timeframe, the rule provides:

> ***(1) A party shall be deemed to admit the authenticity of a document disclosed to him under Part 31 (disclosure and inspection of documents) unless he serves notice that he wishes the document to be proved at trial.***
>
> ***(2) A notice to prove a document must be served –***
>
> > ***(a) by the latest date for serving witness statements; or***
> >
> > ***(b) within 7 days of disclosure of the document, whichever is later.***

If the authenticity of the footage is not challenged, then disclosure of the surveillance file itself should be sufficient for cross-examining purposes. Should the authenticity of the evidence be challenged then the claimant should seek disclosure of all of the surveillance logs and witness statements from all the surveillance operatives who took the various films. It is common to see operatives working in pairs, and as we have seen above, footage may be taken over a sustained period of time. Therefore, there may be multiple witness statements to be prepared and served. If the claimant considers that there are gaps in those statements or areas left unexplained, then they may wish to avail themselves of a request for further information pursuant to CPR 18.

CHAPTER THREE

DISCLOSING SURVEILLANCE EVIDENCE

Once surveillance evidence has been obtained, and the party obtaining it has decided to deploy it, a decision has to be taken as to how and when it is deployed. This needs to be addressed in two stages, firstly the practicalities of how such evidence is disclosed. Secondly, the disclosing party must consider at what stage the evidence should be disclosed. The two points are considered below.

Disclosure of surveillance evidence

The general principle is that it will usually be in the interests of justice for a defendant to be able to rely on surveillance evidence which undermines the claimant's case, and to cross-examine the claimant and their medical experts on it, so long as this does not amount to trial by ambush. As was discussed in chapter one, surveillance evidence is privileged, however, a party who proposes to use surveillance evidence to attack another party's case will waive that privilege when the evidence is disclosed.

The surveillance evidence is often disclosed to the opposing party in the form of edited footage. It should be remembered though that once privilege is waived, it is waived over the whole of the document and therefore the whole document becomes disclosable. Often the first response from the opposing party is to request the complete and unedited footage of all of the surveillance conducted. This can sometimes cause a difficulty, some of the footage may have become corrupted if it is was obtained some time ago, some of it may have been lost and may not be available for disclosure.

Claimants may seek confirmation as to whether the defendant has any other surveillance evidence, as the complete footage may present a picture that is of less assistance to the defendant than the edited footage that has been served. Therefore, the defendant should ensure that all of the footage can be and is retained in order that it may be made available either upon request or upon order of the court.

If the defendant refuses to disclose any additional or the complete surveillance evidence, then that may be a matter for the court to weigh in deciding whether permission should be granted to the defendant to rely on the surveillance evidence as served. Even if permission is granted, then the court at trial may feel itself unable to place much weight on the edited surveillance evidence, given that it does not have the complete evidence to review, an examination of the best evidence rule is contained in chapter one. Whilst not a personal injury claim, some assistance can be gained from the Employment Appeals Tribunal judgment in the case of ***Pendragon Motor Company Ltd t/a Stratstone (Wilmslow) Ltd v Mr A K Ridge [2001] UKEAT 962_00_0511***:

> ***... the Tribunal fell into error in regarding the fact that the video was admittedly a video which had been edited and did not show continuous activity over a period of hours as being a ground for excluding it from consideration altogether. It was agreed that the video evidence sought to be placed before the Tribunal had been edited from a much longer period of video surveillance of Mr Ridge, but it was not disputed before the Tribunal that the edited passages showed a genuine picture of the activities that Mr Ridge was in fact carrying out at the time they were taken...the fact that a video shows edited highlights is quite properly a matter which can be the subject of submission to the Tribunal on the weight to be attached to it. That is a matter on which, obviously, Mr Ridge will be able to give evidence, and submissions can be made on his behalf on the value to be attached to the edited version of the video at the actual hearing itself. But we are not satisfied that that is in itself a ground for refusing to accept it as evidence altogether.***

Parties need to consider how they address the surveillance evidence with their own experts. It is usual practice for the medico-legal experts to examine the footage and comment on the level of physical capability displayed by the claimant. Parties do need to be careful not to compromise their expert by showing them footage upon which they may not have permission to rely. It needs to be remembered that the mere fact that surveillance evidence has been disclosed, and a medico-legal expert has looked at it, does not mean that a court will be obliged to admit the evidence. This may be a factor that the court could take into consideration when reaching its decision as to whether or not to admit the evidence, but it is not determinative of the issue.

Timing of disclosure of surveillance evidence

Perhaps one of the most crucial decisions taken by a party who has obtained surveillance evidence is when to disclose the evidence. By its nature, litigation is a fluid process and the developments in the evidence and the responses of the opposing parties cannot always be anticipated. If evidence is disclosed too early, the responding party may have an opportunity to counter its effect and nullify its impact. If the evidence is disclosed too late, then the court may deny the adducing party permission to rely upon the evidence if it causes too much disruption to the court's timetable and is an attempt at an ambush.

It is fair to say that there is a general principle that it will usually be in the interests of justice for a defendant to be able to rely on surveillance evidence which is relevant to the issues in the case. The defendant should be permitted to cross-examine the claimant and their medical experts on relevant evidence, so long as this does not amount to trial by ambush. This general principle should not be relied upon as a blanket rule that parties can obtain surveillance evidence by any means and disclose it at any stage they want to in a case.

These principles were set out in the court of appeal's judgment in ***Sally Rall v Ross Hulme [2001] EWCA Civ 146***, where it was held that:

> ***In principle, as it seems to me, the starting point on any application of this kind must be that, where video evidence is available which, according to the defendant, undermines the case of the claimant to an extent that would substantially reduce the award of damages to which she is entitled, it will usually be in the overall interests of justice to require that the defendant should***

> ***be permitted to cross-examine the claimant and her medical advisers upon it, so long as this does not amount to trial by ambush. This was not an ambush case: there had been no deliberate delay in disclosure by the defendant so as to achieve surprise, nor was the delay otherwise culpable, bearing in mind the mutual muddle over the 9 October hearing date. Nor is this the comparatively rare kind of case in which the film has to be independently adduced because what it shows goes beyond what can be established by cross-examination, and where different directions may be needed.***

Prior to the introduction of the CPR, the courts allowed the party serving surveillance evidence to ambush the other party, potentially even as late as at trial, with the surveillance footage. This course of conduct started to be discouraged, the court of appeal held in ***Khan (Avrangzeb) v Armaguard Ltd. [1994] 1 W.L.R. 1204 (CA)***, that it would not normally be appropriate to have surveillance evidence withheld until trial so that the opposing party was ambushed by its late disclosure.

With the introduction of the CPR, and the 'cards on the table' approach to litigation the courts have had to re-examine the principles surrounding the timing of disclosure of surveillance evidence as this can be one of the most contentious issues in a case where such evidence is deployed. This has led to the generation of a large amount of first instance and appellate authority on the appropriate timing of disclosure of surveillance evidence.

It may seem somewhat unusual to say it, given that the service of surveillance evidence can lead to an attack on the very credibility of the claimant and raise their ire, but parties are required to co-operate with each other during the litigation process. In the case of ***Hannon v Hillingdon Homes Limited [2013] EWHC 4553 (QB)***, the high court held that:

> ***So, the rules relating to the obtaining and introduction of surveillance evidence are rules which should be applied by the case manager so as so far as possible so as to comply with the overriding objective and with a litigant's rights, particularly his right to a private and family life. The parties are, moreover,***

> ***required to cooperate with each other in the litigation in order to ensure, as far as is possible, fairness to both parties and to all parties in the litigation.***

Therefore, upon service of the surveillance evidence parties should be examining how they can co-operate to accommodate the developments in the litigation. A failure to do so can lead to the court penalising a recalcitrant party. In ***Stewart v Kelly [2016] EWHC 3263 (QB)***, the court found that the defendant was entitled to see how the claimant 'pinned his colours to the mast' in the witness statements relied upon by the claimant. Having done so, there was a duty to then act briskly in deciding whether to commission further surveillance evidence. In ***Stewart*** the court found that the claimant had no good objection to the surveillance evidence being admitted, and they had failed to work promptly to agree new directions that might have enabled the trial date to be kept. It is important to note in this judgment that the court was critical of the claimant for not working to agree new directions. It is an indicator that the claimant cannot simply ignore the evidence and not consider how it impacts upon the case.

Due to the secretive way in which the evidence is gathered and the need for surprise in its disclosure, the defendant will wish the claimant to have committed to their case before the evidence is served. This can often be seen by the defendant waiting for the claimant to serve a witness statement with a signed statement of truth before it serves its surveillance evidence. In this statement it is common to see the claimant setting out their case as to their level of functional capabilities, working capacities and evidence as to how the accident-related injuries have affected them. In the case of ***Uttely v Uttley [2001] Lexis Citation 1948***, Hallett J (as she then was) held that:

> ***the defendant's solicitors were entitled to press for an up-to-date witness statement and schedule, and to press for documents of that kind in the summer of 2000. They were entitled to know what the claimant was saying himself, not merely what he had reported to [the medical expert].***

This decision was underscored by the judgment in ***Katrina Draper v Nottingham City Council [2017] 11 WLUK 644*** where, on appeal in the County Court, HHJ Owen QC held that:

> ***It was not unreasonable for it to wish to ensure that the claimant, who it suspected of malingering, had nailed her colours to the mast before the disclosure of such evidence. However, it was a question of judgement and degree as to when such disclosure should be made. The longer it was left and the nearer it was to the trial, the greater the risk of refusal on the grounds of unfairness and ambush. Where it appeared, or was plain, that the defendant was engaged in tactical late disclosure designed to prevent the claimant from having an adequate opportunity in which to deal with such evidence without a good forensic purpose or reason for the delay, the court would refuse the application to ensure that the claim could be presented by both parties fairly, even if that meant excluding relevant evidence. Conversely, where there was a legitimate reason for a defendant not to reveal its hand at that particular stage, notwithstanding that there was a fixed trial date, it did not necessarily follow that that delay in disclosure was conduct amounting to ambush and thus illegitimate tactical manoeuvring.***

A further foundation case in this area is that of ***Tavenor Joe Douglas (A Protected Party By his Litigation Friend William Robertson) v Matthew James O'Neill [2011] EWHC 601 (QB)***, where the defendant served surveillance evidence approximately three months prior to the trial. The reason for the defendant withholding the evidence until that point was that the claimant had failed to serve his witness statement and certain elements of his expert evidence. The court held that the defendant was entitled to wait until the claimant had served his signed witness statement and that the evidence had been disclosed at the first reasonable opportunity. The court stated at para 46 of the judgment:

> ***In my judgment the issue of ambush comes to this -are the circumstances in which the evidence is disclosed such that the Claimant has a fair opportunity to deal with it, or was the time or circumstances of disclosure such that the court should use its***

> ***case management powers to prevent the defendant from relying upon it?***

And at para 56 stated:

> ***...a defendant in possession of surveillance evidence should make the decision to rely upon it and disclose it as soon as reasonably possible after receiving sufficient material setting out the Claimant's case, which has been endorsed with a statement of truth so as to enable the surveillance material to be used effectively. If a defendant fails to do so, and the failure to do so has unacceptable case management implications, then that defendant risks being unable to rely upon the material.***

As can be seen from these authorities, the defendant is entitled to wait until the claimant has pinned their colours to the mast before they disclose surveillance evidence. The defendant cannot wait until the last moment to serve its evidence, and choosing the exact moment of disclosure is a tactical consideration that must be weighed according to the facts of each case.

The decision about when to obtain the evidence though can impact on when evidence is served. In some cases, surveillance evidence is obtained in the pre-action stages or the early stages of the litigation, but this is not always either practical or necessary. In ***Watson v Ministry of Defence [2016] EWHC 3163 (QB)***, the defendant had delayed in obtaining the surveillance footage. The defendant had obtained the footage when it became clear that it would be relevant, and this was not until much later in the case than would normally be seen. On the facts of the case the judge did not consider that admitting the video footage would result in an ambush at trial. The point for the court to consider is whether there was a reasonable suspicion for the defendant to act upon for them to have acquired the surveillance evidence earlier.

The issue of the timing of disclosure was examined more recently in the case of ***Grant v Newport City Council [2018] EWHC 3813 Ch***. In this case the defendant initially obtained footage of the claimant walking, and further surveillance then demonstrated her working. This was all contrary to the claimant's pleaded case. Approximately four weeks before trial, the defendant disclosed the surveillance evidence and applied for permission to rely on the same and to amend its defence to plead fraud.

At first instance, the court dismissed the application on the grounds that allowing the evidence would require the trial date to be vacated, and the defendant had delayed in making its application to rely upon the surveillance evidence.

On appeal, Birss J considered the date on which the defendant should have disclosed the surveillance footage. The defendant monitored the claimant in February 2018 and then again in March 2018. The footage was disclosed to the claimant in June 2018. Birss J held that:

> ***the defendant could and should have disclosed the February footage at that stage … if it wanted to ensure there was no risk of procedural unfairness to the claimant…***

Next, the court considered whether or not the trial had to be adjourned if permission to rely upon the footage was granted. The submission that the trial should be adjourned if the defendant could have paid the claimant's costs thrown away was rejected, the payment of costs did not justify the vacation of a trial date. In addition, the court accepted the claimant's submission that the four weeks between the application hearing and trial would not have been sufficient for the claimant to compile her own evidence and respond effectively to the surveillance footage.

Despite the unsatisfactory situation, the court noted that the trial date had been lost pending the appeal anyway. The claimant therefore now had an opportunity to address the surveillance footage and take whatever staps she needed to respond to it. The surveillance evidence was therefore admitted.

The judgment highlights the principle that surveillance evidence must be deployed at a point in time that is unlikely to cause much disruption to the litigation timetable. A timetable will less likely be endangered if the surveillance evidence is served at the time of exchange of witness statements, as this development in the litigation usually takes place well in advance of trial. This does have a drawback for the defendant though, because litigators are compelled to decide very early on whether or not to obtain surveillance evidence. It should also be borne in mind from the decision, that although the surveillance evidence was eventually admitted, that was solely a matter of practicality, it cannot be taken as an authority that such evidence will always be allowed in other claims. The case also reminds litigators that payment of costs for a vacated trial is no justification for late disclosure.

Ambushes & late applications

We have looked above at the ideal timing of disclosure of surveillance evidence, those instances discuss how evidence would be disclosed in an 'perfect' piece of litigation. Not every case is ideal though, sometimes new information will come to light post exchange of witness evidence which will cause a defendant to consider it is appropriate to gather surveillance evidence for the first time, as was seen above in ***Watson***. This next section examines how courts approach the issue of late applications to rely upon surveillance evidence.

Late applications can have significant repercussions for defendants. In ***Lorna Catherine Hayden v Maidstone & Tunbridge Wells NHS Trust*** *[2016] EWHC 1121 (QB)*, the court had 'considerable misgivings' about allowing late surveillance evidence and the evidence was only admitted in the overall interests of justice. The defendant did fall liable for the costs of the trial that had to be vacated because of the admittance of the surveillance evidence and in addition the costs of the application, these costs were ordered to be paid on the indemnity basis, along with the costs that the claimant was going to incur in additional costs of the experts having to consider the new evidence. As such a defendant must carefully weigh the considerations of the importance of the evidence against the possible consequences of its, potential, late admittance.

When determining an application regarding surveillance evidence, the court has to ask itself whether or not the conduct of the defendant does amount to an attempt at ambush or not. What actually constitutes an ambush will be fact specific, but in ***Douglas*** and in ***Rall***, the court gave some guidance and stated:

> *This was not an "ambush" case: there had been no deliberate delay in disclosure by the defendant so as to achieve surprise, nor was the delay otherwise culpable.*

and

> *In my judgment the issue of ambush comes to this—are the circumstances in which the evidence is disclosed such that the Claimant has a fair opportunity to deal with it, or was the time or circumstances of disclosure such that the court should use its case management powers to prevent the defendant from relying upon it?*

The latitude given to defendants to conceal the fact and content of surveillance evidence until the circumstances allow it to be most effectively deployed, does not excuse them from their obligations under the overriding objective. In ***Hannon***, the court held:

> *...it was clearly of particular importance for those managing the case preparation and the pre-trial steps on behalf of both parties to coordinate the various steps being taken and to maintain the timetable that had been crafted in order to give effect to those steps. This was because a balance would need to be struck between, on the one hand, maintaining the timetable and, on the other hand, the obtaining of evidence without the claimant being aware that it was being obtained, but with disclosure of that evidence taking place so that the claimant was not prejudiced. Moreover, the case manager for the time needed to be fully appraised of the situation so as to give effect to the overriding objective...the rules relating to the obtaining and introduction of surveillance evidence are rules which should be applied by the case manager so as so far as possible so as to comply with the overriding objective and with a litigant's rights, particularly his right to a private and family life. The parties are, moreover, required to cooperate with each other in the litigation in order to ensure, as far as is possible, fairness to both parties and to all parties in the litigation.*

As we examined above, in the case of ***Hayden***, the high court reiterated the principle that the courts do not tolerate trial by ambush. In this case, the claimant had brought a claim for injury and loss arising from an accident at work. The defendant obtained surveillance evidence but at a time when the trial window had been listed and was approaching. Furthermore, the defendant only issued its application seeking permission to rely upon the evidence, around six days prior to the claimant giving evidence at trial. The high court reluctantly allowed the surveillance footage to be relied upon. The trial date was vacated but the defendant was required to pay the wasted costs of this and also of the claimant's expert's additional costs of considering the new evidence. In giving judgment, Foskett J drew a distinction between when surveillance ought to be commissioned and when it ought to be disclosed. He stated that:

> ***A very significant factor in deciding whether to accede to a late application, in my judgment, is the time when a defendant ought reasonably to commission such evidence. Once the claimant's case, both in relation to the disabilities relied upon and their consequences, is clearly articulated and the defendant is possessed of an opinion from an expert upon whom it relies that the claim is "suspect", it seems to me that the obligation actively to obtain surveillance evidence arises if it is considered a proportionate approach to adopt in the particular case. The longer it is left and the nearer the time gets to trial, the more likely it is that the court will regard the delay as culpable.***

In addressing the issue of ambush, Foskett J held that more liberal use might be made of court orders containing a 'date by which' direction. This would require surveillance evidence to be served by a set date, if it has been obtained. If the defendant breached such a direction and then sought to rely upon surveillance evidence, this would then engage the relief from sanctions considerations and require any application to deploy the evidence to be assessed by reference to the ***Denton v TH White Ltd [2014] EWCA Civ 906*** approach, which is discussed in more detail below. Foskett J considered that, once a defendant had an expert opinion which gave it reasonable cause to suspect that surveillance evidence ought to be obtained, there was an obligation to obtain surveillance evidence with due expedition if that was considered a proportionate approach. The longer it was left and the nearer it got to trial, the more likely it was that the delay would be held culpable and permission to rely upon the evidence would be refused.

In ***Dass v Dass [2013] EWHC 2520 (QB)***, the court considered that if a defendant makes a tactical decision not to serve its expert evidence in time, but to benefit from the delay to obtain surveillance evidence then it risks being refused permission to rely on expert evidence served late, even where there has been inaction by the claimant and the trial date would not be affected.

It might be felt by claimants that the line of authorities in this area is against them and that they are often the victims of ambushes by surveillance footage. For example, in ***Hicks v Rostas and Motor Insurance Bureau High Court (QB) His Honour Judge Reddihough 17 March 2017***, the high court allowed the defendant's surveillance evidence to be relied upon despite the application only being heard one month from trial. It cannot be said that every application for permission to rely upon surveillance evidence will be granted and the court will not permit an attempt at trial by ambush. In ***O'Leary v Tunnelcraft Ltd [2009] EWHC 3438 (QB)***, the court refused permission to a defendant who sought to rely upon surveillance evidence that it had disclosed.

The chronology and the background to the court's case management is worthy of review because of the early case management directions. On 3 May 2007, at a directions hearing, the high court Master ordered, amongst other things, that any application by the defendant to rely upon surveillance evidence should be made no later than 1 July 2008. No surveillance evidence was disclosed prior to that date or thereafter because it was stated that no such evidence had been obtained at that stage.

It is appropriate to pause at this stage to note the active case management taken by the high court Master at the interlocutory stage. The court has a wide range of case management powers open to it pursuant to ***CPR 3.1(2)***, to make directions to further the overriding objective. The laying down of a set date by which surveillance evidence was to be served is an example of how the court can control the evidence in a claim, and it echoes the position set out by Foskett J in ***Hannon***, which was discussed above.

The defendant did not serve the surveillance evidence in compliance with the directions order and applied at a later date for permission to rely upon its surveillance footage. Swift J heard the application on 10 November 2009, 31 days from the start of the trial window, the trial itself was listed for six days. The court noted that, in June 2009, the claimant's schedule of loss was served, this schedule included a large claim for both past and future losses. It was not until this stage that the defendant began to obtain surveillance evidence. In determining the application, Swift J said that she considered that this case was an ambush, and that there was no reason why the surveillance footage should not have been disclosed earlier.

Given the order made by the Master at the interlocutory stage, if the court does adopt a 'date by' stance, and the defendant breaches the provisions then relief from sanctions may be required. Pursuant to ***CPR 3.9***:

> ***(1) On an application for relief from any sanction imposed for a failure to comply with any rule, practice direction or court order, the court will consider all the circumstances of the case, so as to enable it to deal justly with the application, including the need –***
>
> > ***(a) for litigation to be conducted efficiently and at proportionate cost; and***
> >
> > ***(b) to enforce compliance with rules, practice directions and orders.***
>
> ***(2) An application for relief must be supported by evidence.***

In considering relief from sanctions the test to be applied by the court is set out in ***Denton*** (mentioned above). This requires that the defaulting party will need to identify whether:

1. The breach of the time limit is serious and significant;

2. The reason for the time limit being breached;

3. In all the circumstances of the case should the application be allowed to proceed.

For the defendant this adds the additional hurdle when making a late application when a 'date by' order also exists, to not only address the issue of a potential ambush, but also as to why relief from sanctions should be granted.

It is important for the parties to remember that, in their discussions about varying directions to accommodate the surveillance evidence, they do not have the power to consent to vacating a trial date. The vacation of a trial date is the preserve of the court and not the parties, and for any party to take the position that late disclosure can be excused on the basis of the trial date being vacated is a fallacy.

During trial

It would not be right to conclude this chapter without making reference to the rare circumstances seen in the case of ***Ford v GKR Construction Ltd and others [2000] 1 All ER***. In this case, the claimant brought an action for personal injury arising from a road traffic accident. The trial to assess damages commenced on 17 September 1998 but was adjourned the next day. Following the adjournment, the defendants decided for the first time to obtain surveillance evidence, and this cast doubt on the veracity of the claimant's claim. During the resumed hearing, the judge allowed the defendants to adduce the video evidence and late medical evidence.

It may seem at odds with many of the cases discussed above to have permission for fundamental evidence to be given once the trial has started, but in ***Ford***, the period of adjournment weighed heavily in favour of permission being granted as this allowed the claimant the opportunity to respond to it.

CHAPTER FOUR

COUNTER EVIDENCE

After surveillance evidence has been served, the receiving party will consider the evidence, its effect on their case, and their response to the evidence. While adverse surveillance evidence is likely to be damaging to a claimant's pleaded case, it is not necessarily fatal, ultimately, it is a matter of fact and degree.

How a claimant responds to surveillance evidence will depend upon what the claimant's pleaded case actually is, what is seen on the footage itself and how, if at all that contradicts the claim, how the footage was obtained, the extent of the footage and its quality and are all important considerations. This chapter examines how a claimant may seek to respond to the footage that has been disclosed.

Association of British Insurers guidance

An early consideration is whether the admissibility of the footage should be challenged. The receiving party will often consider how the surveillance evidence was obtained and whether it was obtained improperly. The case law in relation to improperly obtained evidence was discussed in chapter two. When a claimant considers the evidence and their response, it is not unusual to consider in their reply, the guidance that the Association of British Insurers ('ABI') has provided in this regard. The ABI has drafted a Code of Ethics and Professional Standards which sets out the foundation principles of the ABI's ethical beliefs. Whilst a breach of its principles is not necessarily binding on a court when considering an application for permission to rely upon surveillance evidence, it is persuasive information.

There are two founding principles that become relevant when considering how to respond to surveillance evidence. ***Principle 4*** provides:

> ***All members of The Association of British Investigators are to obey the law and refrain from carrying out any act that they know, or ought to know, is unlawful, or contrary to The Association's policy. All members are expected to challenge and when appropriate, take action and formally report breaches of this code and the improper conduct of other professionals.***

In addition, ***Principle 7*** provides:

> ***All members The Association of British Investigators are to act in a professional manner. They must not behave in a manner which brings, or is likely to bring, discredit upon The Association or any of their clients, or act in a way that undermines or is likely to undermine confidence in The Association or that of any of their or the members' clients, or breach or permit a breach of The Association's Memorandum, Articles of Association, Bye-Laws or Code of Ethics & Professional Standards.***

The party responding to the surveillance evidence therefore should consider if the evidence has been obtained in breach of these principles and the principles discussed in chapter two. They can then consider whether they wish to take issue with this either in response to the evidence, or before the court at a contested application hearing.

Claimant's evidence in reply

The starting point for the claimant to consider is whether or not they actually wish to challenge the surveillance evidence and the content of the footage. If the surveillance evidence depicts the claimant's true functional capabilities, then the claimant may choose not to respond to the disclosed footage. Such consideration needs to be taken upon careful reflection of the entirety of the evidence in the case.

If the claimant is going to contest the evidence, then the claimant is deemed to admit the authenticity of the film unless they serve notice pursuant to ***CPR 32.19*** that they wish the evidence to be proved at trial, as outlined in chapter one. If the claimant does not challenge the authenticity of the footage, it is available to the defendant for the purposes of cross-examining the claimant and/or the claimant's expert medical witnesses at court, unless the court orders otherwise. If such notice is served the defendant should serve a witness statement by the person/s who took the footage in order to prove its authenticity. The issue of proving admissible evidence was discussed in chapter one.

If the claimant consents to the defendant relying on the surveillance evidence or the court permits the evidence, the claimant will likely consider seeking permission to have their own medical experts provide supplementary reports in reply to the evidence. It is common to see these issues addressed at an interlocutory hearing whereby the defendant seeks to rely upon the footage and the claimant seeks permission to adduce further evidence to respond to the footage. Often a claimant will seek to have their own medical experts examine the footage and confirm how, if at all, it affects their conclusions, and the claimant will seek to serve a further witness statement addressing the content of the surveillance footage.

At an interlocutory hearing, if the defendant is granted permission to rely upon surveillance evidence, the court will consider whether any further directions need to be put into place. A common direction to see is for permission to be given to serve addendum expert evidence from the medico-legal experts in the case as to their opinion regarding the surveillance footage. If permission is given to address the surveillance evidence, then any evidence served needs to be kept within the boundaries of the court's order. This issue was examined in the case of ***Jason Tully v (1) Exterion Media (UK) Ltd (In Liquidation) (2) London Underground Ltd [2020] EWHC 1119 (QB)***, Master McCloud had to consider the issue of relief from sanctions when addressing the claimant's response to the surveillance evidence served by the defendant. The defendant contended that the claimant had strayed outside of the limits set by the court's order when serving evidence in response to the surveillance footage, and that the additional evidence should be excluded. The court held that:

> ***The claimant, who had permission under a court order for a further exchange of expert medical reports "limited to issues arising from the [defendants'] surveillance footage and [his] witness statement", had breached the order where his orthopaedic expert had re-examined him and produced an***

> ***updating report which dealt generally with his medical position. He was entitled to only limited relief from sanctions.***

Parties should therefore be careful that only evidence relating to the surveillance footage is served in response to it.

If the claimant wishes to serve a further witness statement, the same often addresses the claimant's areas of disagreement in relation to the surveillance evidence and how their functional capabilities differ from the footage that has been recorded. Sometimes such statements will set out a 'day in life of' the claimant and how the injuries typically affect the claimant each day. The issue for the claimant therefore is to ensure that the amended directions order provides them with enough scope to be able to respond adequately to the surveillance evidence.

Counter surveillance report

If a defendant serves surveillance evidence it is not uncommon for them to receive in response, not only a request for all of the unedited surveillance footage, but a report from a video surveillance operative. Such a report will likely seek to comment upon how the footage was probably obtained, any areas of discrepancy in the recording methodology, whether the film has been speeded up at any stage, and whether there are any sections missing.

In determining whether the claimant should have permission to rely upon such a report, there are competing authorities to consider, the first is ***Marlene Samson v Mohammed Ali [2012] EWHC 4146 (QB).*** In this case the claimant advanced a claim for injury and loss following a road traffic collision. The claimant alleged that she was seriously restricted in her ability to move because of a knee injury sustained in the accident. The defendant served surveillance evidence that they alleged demonstrated that the claimant's range of movement was much greater than that alleged.

The claimant served a report which sought to cast doubt on whether all of the surveillance footage had been disclosed. In addition, it was contended that the footage had, in places, been 'speeded up' to give the impression that the claimant was moving more freely than she was in fact doing. The court allowed the evidence of the counter-surveillance report finding that it would be helpful evidence for the trial judge to hear.

Some doubt has been cast on ***Samson*** by ***Lorna Catherine Hayden v Maidstone & Tunbridge Wells NHS Trust [2016] EWHC 1121 (QB).*** In ***Hayden***, the claimant brought a claim for personal injury and losses arising from a back injury sustained at work. The defendant served surveillance evidence that sought to undermine the claimant's position and the claimant served a report from a video analysis consultant.

The court held that the opinion evidence of the counter surveillance operative should be excluded, but that the factual analysis contained within some of the appendices to the report would be helpful for the trial judge to consider. The opinion evidence though did not assist the court and many of the issues were factual matters which were the remit of the trial judge, as such the report in this regard was excluded.

Of further relevance also is the judgment of HHJ Keyser QC in the county court at Cardiff in the case of ***Chadwick v Lewis & Aviva Insurance Ltd [2016]***, where HHJ Keyser QC warned against a 'cottage industry' being brought into existence by the use of counter surveillance reports and that this would make issues relating to surveillance evidence more difficult for the court than they already are.

It would be wrong to say that counter surveillance reports will now be excluded in light of ***Hayden*** and ***Chadwick***. In ***Samson***, the court clearly found assistance from the reports in relation to the technical issue about the footage being speeded up, but in ***Hayden***, the court found that the report did little more than analyse areas that the trial judge needed to make factual findings on. The key issue is perhaps whether the court can derive from the report assistance that it would not otherwise find from the remaining evidence before it.

Expert evidence

Before addressing whether a counter-surveillance report is expert evidence or not, it must be remembered that courts cannot and do not simply allow parties to rely upon whatever expert evidence they wish. The courts control the provision of expert evidence through the CPR. The starting principle is ***CPR 35.1*** which provides:

> ***Expert evidence shall be restricted to that which is reasonably required to resolve the proceedings.***

In ***R v Bonython (1984) 38 SASR 45***, the court found that:

> ***If on the proven facts a judge or jury can form their own conclusions without help, then the opinion of an expert is unnecessary.***

In that regard, ***CPR 35.4(1)*** provides:

> ***No party may call an expert or put in evidence an expert's report without the court's permission.***

The courts therefore keep very tight control on what expert evidence is allowed in cases and expert evidence shall be restricted to that which is reasonably required to resolve the proceedings. In addressing the issue of whether counter surveillance reports are expert reports or not, the court set out the starting point in the case of ***Barings plc v Coopers & Lybrand [2001] PNLR 22***, this provides the following test:

> ***the test whether expert evidence in any particular case is to be received is a two stage test, the first stage being whether the evidence is admissible as 'expert evidence' for the purposes of section 3 of the 1972 Act, and the second stage whether the Court should admit it as being relevant to any decision which the Court has to arrive at, that is, helpful to the Court for that purpose.***

The court added that:

> ***expert evidence is admissible under section 3 of the Civil Evidence Act 1972 in any case where the Court accepts that there exists a recognised expertise governed by recognised standards and rules of conduct capable of influencing the Court's decision on any of the issues which it has to decide and the witness to be called satisfies the Court that he has a sufficient familiarity with and knowledge of the expertise in question to render his opinion***

> ***potentially of value in resolving any of those issues. Evidence meeting this test can still be excluded by the Court if the Court takes the view that calling it will not be helpful to the Court in resolving any issue in the case justly. Such evidence will not be helpful where the issue to be decided is one of law or is otherwise one on which the Court is able to come to a fully informed decision without hearing such evidence.***

The court therefore has to consider whether the report will be of assistance to the trial judge, as in ***Samson*** where the report addressed areas requiring technical expertise, or was it an analysis of factual matters that were the remit of the trial judge, as in ***Hayden***. In determining whether a report can be admitted, the court will consider who can be classified as an 'expert'. ***CPR 35.2(1)*** provides:

> ***A reference to an 'expert' in this Part is a reference to a person who has been instructed to give or prepare expert evidence for the purpose of proceedings.***

Pursuant to ***CPR 35 Practice Direction 3.2(1)***:

> ***An expert's report must:***
>
> ***(1) give details of the expert's qualifications;***

The above provisions of the CPR do not give much assistance to the court in determining who is an expert, and qualifications do not necessarily equate to expertise. A person claiming to be an expert in a field will have to satisfy the court that they have the requisite skills and knowledge to provide a valid opinion. In ***Kennedy v Cordia Services (LLP) [2016] UKSC 6***, the supreme court gave guidance as to the need to regulate skilled witness evidence.

By way of background, the claimant worked for the defendant as a home carer. On 18 December 2010, she slipped and fell on an icy footpath leading to the home of one of her clients, and she sustained an injury to her wrist. The defendant had carried out risk assessments which identified the danger of falls when employees were travelling between work locations. The defendant had not considered the possibility of issuing its employees with anti-slip attachments designed to increase traction in icy conditions, which became relevant later on in the proceedings.

The claimant brought a claim for personal injury that was heard in the Outer House of the Scottish Court of Session. The claimant served a report from and relied upon the evidence of Mr Greasly, an engineering consultant who had experience in advising companies on health and safety risks. This evidence commented upon the risk assessments carried out by the defendant, and disagreed with the categorisation of the risk of employees falling and sustaining injury in these circumstances. The evidence also explained that a number of employers provided such anti-slip attachments which reduced the risk of falls on snow or ice.

The defendant objected to the admission of Mr Greasly's evidence on the basis that he did not have any relevant special skill to qualify him to act as a skilled witness, this argument was rejected. The court found that the defendant's risk assessments had been inadequate, there had been a failure to take relatively simple precautions to reduce the risk of injury to the claimant, and the defendant was liable for the claimant's losses.

The case reached the supreme court, and some of the grounds for this are outside of the remit of this text, but in addressing the issue of expert evidence, the court recognised the need to regulate skilled witness evidence, acknowledging that it can be very influential, and difficult for the other party to test unless assisted by expert advice themselves. The court set our four considerations governing the admissibility of skilled evidence:

> ***(i) whether the proposed skilled evidence will assist the court in its task;***
>
> ***(ii) whether the witness has the necessary knowledge and experience;***
>
> ***(iii) whether the witness is impartial in his or her presentation and assessment of the evidence; and***

> ***(iv) whether there is a reliable body of knowledge or experience to underpin the expert's evidence.***

In ***Samson***, the counter-surveillance report advanced the position that elements of the video evidence had been omitted or had been withheld. In addition, the video evidence that had been served had been 'speeded up' in order to portray a different functional position to that which the claimant had advanced. As seen above, this point was one of technical analysis which the court found would be assisted by the counter-surveillance report.

This does raise the practical issue for lawyers who serve surveillance evidence, as, prior to the disclosure of the same, it is prudent to subject the report, and possibly the agents who obtained it, to critical scrutiny. This can ensure that the evidence cannot be criticised or, under analysis from a counter-surveillance agent, denigrated.

The key question is, does the evidence add anything to the proceedings that the trial judge cannot glean for themselves from watching the surveillance footage. Is the evidence expert evidence or is the evidence an analysis of factual material which would be the remit of the trial judge. If the evidence falls into the latter category, then it is more likely to be rejected and no permission given to rely upon it.

CHAPTER FIVE

USE OF SURVEILLANCE EVIDENCE AT TRIAL

As practitioners know, many cases do not reach trial. After service of all of the evidence, especially surveillance evidence that has a significant effect on the claim, the case may settle, be withdrawn or in extreme instances, be struck out. If the case does proceed to trial, then the parties need to address how the effect of the surveillance evidence is managed in the approach to, and at, the trial.

It may seem a rather obvious point but is something that can be overlooked in the perhaps frenetic preparations for trial, but communication with the court office is extremely important to ensure that facilities are available at trial for the surveillance footage to be played. It is somewhat embarrassing for litigants to enter a court with what may be, crucial video evidence only to find that the court office has not been notified of the need to have facilities available for the court to examine the evidence.

Statements of case

An early consideration following the disclosure of the surveillance evidence, and in preparation for trial, is whether any party needs to make an application to amend a statement of case. From the defendant's perspective a consideration may need to be taken as to whether it may now be appropriate to positively plead that the claim is fraudulent.

If any party is to make an application to amend a statement of case, then the party needs either the court's permission to amend the statement of case or needs the written consent of all of the parties. *CPR 17.1(2)* provides:

> **(2) If his statement of case has been served, a party may amend it only –**

(a) with the written consent of all the other parties; or

(b) with the permission of the court.

Without the written consent of the parties or the court's permission, the court has the power to disallow the amendments pursuant to ***CPR 17.2***. When considering whether an application to amend a statement of case should be granted, the court will have regard to the Notes to ***CPR 17.3***.

Applications to amend statements of case require the court to strike a balance between injustice to the applicant if the application is refused, and injustice to the respondent if the amendment is permitted. One of the key considerations for the court is whether the proposed amendments have a reasonable prospect of success. In ***SPR North Ltd v Swiss Post International (UK) Ltd [2019] EWHC 2004 (Ch)*** the court held that the test to be applied in an application to amend a statement of case, is the same as the test applied to an application for summary judgment, ie. whether the proposed statement of case has a real prospect of success. This approach is re-in forced by the court's decision in ***Groveholt Ltd v Hughes [2010] EWCA Civ 538***, where an application for permission to amend a defence was refused when it was clear that the proposed amendment had no prospect of success.

A further important consideration is the stage in the litigation when the application is made, by necessity this issue will have similar considerations to the timing of when the surveillance evidence is disclosed. In ***CIP Properties (AIPT) Ltd v Galliford Try Infrastructure Ltd [2015] EWHC 1345 (TCC)***, the court found that the question of whether an amendment could have been sought earlier, should not be eclipsed by the potential importance of the arguments advanced by the amendment. Therefore, if the defendant's surveillance evidence is fundamental to the case, this would weigh in favour of an application to amend the defence being granted, even of the application could have been brought earlier.

If the application is brought very close to the trial date, the court has to take into account any possible effect that granting the application would have on the trial date, and whether granting the amendment will put the parties on an unequal footing. The Notes to CPR 17.3 set out that a very late amendment is defined as one made when the trial date has been fixed and where the grant of permission to amend would cause the trial date to be lost. In these circumstances, and pursuant to ***Quah v Goldman Sachs International [2015] EWHC 759 (Comm)***, a heavy burden lies upon a party seeking to amend their statement of case at this stage. An explanation must be provided as to why the application was not made earlier, and the applicant must show the strength of the new case.

Ethics & codes of conduct

The following section considers the issue of advancing a positive case of fraud in the amended statement of case. This is considered both from an ethical and a factual perspective. In order to plead an allegation a party needs to know what evidence there is to support the allegation. From an ethical perspective, a chartered legal executive, solicitor or barrister has to consider the relevant code of conduct when advancing their position. The Chartered Institute of Legal Executive's code of conduct provides that the legal executive must:

1.1 ***Understand and comply with your primary and overriding duty to the court, obey court orders and do nothing which would place you in contempt.***

1.2 ***Not knowingly or recklessly allow the court to be misled.***

2.2 ***Not engage in any conduct that could undermine or affect adversely the confidence and trust placed in you and your profession by your client, your employer, professional colleagues, the public and others.***

3.1 ***Be honest in all your dealings and in all financial matters.***

3.2 ***Not intentionally mislead anyone you deal with.***

The Solicitors Regulation Authority code of conduct provides:

1.4 ***You do not mislead or attempt to mislead your clients, the court or others, either by your own acts or omissions or allowing or being complicit in the acts or omissions of others (including your client).***

Should counsel be drafting the statement of case then counsel has to consider the Bar Standards Board Handbook, which provides:

CD1 *You must observe your duty to the court in the administration of justice*

C1 *The court is able to rely on information provided to it by those conducting litigation and by advocates who appear before it.*

C2 *The proper administration of justice is served.*

rC3 *You owe a duty to the court to act with independence in the interests of justice. This duty overrides any inconsistent obligations which you may have (other than obligations under the criminal law). It includes the following specific obligations which apply whether you are acting as an advocate or are otherwise involved in the conduct of litigation in whatever role (with the exception of Rule C3.1 below, which applies when acting as an advocate):*

2 *you must not knowingly or recklessly mislead or attempt to mislead the court;*

3 *you must not abuse your role as an advocate;*

4 *you must take reasonable steps to avoid wasting the court's time; .4 you must take reasonable steps to ensure that the court has before it all relevant decisions and legislative provisions;*

rC6 *Your duty not to mislead the court will include the following obligations:*

1 *you must not:*

(a) *make submissions, representations or any other statement; or*

(b) ask questions which suggest facts to witnesses which you know, or are instructed, are untrue or misleading.

2 you must not call witnesses to give evidence or put affidavits or witness statements to the court which you know, or are instructed, are untrue or misleading, unless you make clear to the court the true position as known by or instructed to you.

gC4 As to your duty not to mislead the court:

1 knowingly misleading the court includes being complicit in another person misleading the court;

2 knowingly misleading the court also includes inadvertently misleading the court if you later realise that you have misled the court, and you fail to correct the position;

3 recklessly means being indifferent to the truth, or not caring whether something is true or false; and

4 the duty continues to apply for the duration of the case.

rC7 .3 you must not make a serious allegation against any person, or suggest that a person is guilty of a crime with which your client is charged unless:

a you have reasonable grounds for the allegation; and

b the allegation is relevant to your client's case or the credibility of a witness; and

c where the allegation relates to a third party, you avoid naming them in open court unless this is reasonably necessary.

rC9 Your duty to act with honesty and with integrity under CD3 includes the following requirements:

1 you must not knowingly or recklessly mislead or attempt to mislead anyone;

2 you must not draft any statement of case, witness statement, affidavit or other document containing:

a any statement of fact or contention which is not supported by your client or by your instructions;

b any contention which you do not consider to be properly arguable;

c any allegation of fraud, unless you have clear instructions to allege fraud and you have reasonably credible material which establishes an arguable case of fraud;

d (in the case of a witness statement or affidavit) any statement of fact other than the evidence which you reasonably believe the witness would give if the witness were giving evidence orally;

Whether someone is acting for a claimant or a defendant there are common themes that can be taken from these codes of conduct. Parties cannot act in contempt of court, from a claimant's perspective, if a claim is so egregiously fraudulent, the claimant's legal representatives may wish to consider if they feel they can still represent the claimant.

Parties must be honest without intentionally misleading anyone and cannot be complicit in an attempt to mislead the court or other parties. This can be applicable to both the claimant and defendant, as the claimant cannot advance a claim to be fraudulent, and a defendant cannot attempt to advance a defence that is not supported by the evidence in the surveillance footage.

Lastly there must be credible material to support an arguable case if fraud is to be alleged. From the defendant's perspective the allegation of fraud can be one of the most explosive allegations to make. If it fails it can lead to costs sanctions being imposed by a court, and the evidence needs to be present in order to support the allegation.

Civil Procedure Rules

Whether a claimant will wish to revise their approach to the claim upon viewing the surveillance footage will depend on whether the footage shows any significant discrepancies between the as seen functional capabilities of the claimant, and the pleaded claim. In relation to the defendant's position, if the defendant is seeking to amend its defence, then pursuant to ***CPR 16.5***, a defendant has to state which allegations are admitted, denied and which allegations he is unable to admit or deny, ***CPR 16.5(3)*** provides:

> ***(3) A defendant who –***
>
> > ***(a) fails to deal with an allegation; but***
> >
> > ***(b) has set out in his defence the nature of his case in relation to the issue to which that allegation is relevant,***
>
> ***shall be taken to require that allegation to be proved.***

How then does a defendant approach a case where the evidence may not be sufficient to positively plead a case of fraud, but where the surveillance footage shows the claimant's level of functional capabilities to be wider than that pleaded. The defendant may feel that they are trapped between the need to positively plead as strong a case as possible, and a need not to fall foul of the ethical requirements not to plead a case of fraud where the evidence does not support such an allegation.

The court of appeal held in ***Alan Mark Kearsely v Daniel Klarfield [2005] EWCA Civ 1510***, that it was sufficient to set out fully any facts from which the defence would be inviting the judge to draw the inference that the claimant had not in fact suffered the injuries he asserted, and that there was no burden on the defence to prove fraud. The defendant does not have to put forward a substantive case of fraud in order to succeed so long as they adhere to ***CPR 16.5***.

It does not follow that when confronted with surveillance evidence the court's decision is binary, the court does not have to either allow the claim in full or make a finding of fraud in order to dismiss the claim. The court has a third option in so far as it can find that the claimant has not overcome the burden of proof in relation to some or all of the heads of damage claimed.

In ***(1) Mr Mohamed Rizan (2) Mr Mohamed Rilshad v (1) Barry Hayes (2) Allianz Insurance Plc [2016] EWCA Civ 481***, the first and second claimants brought proceedings for personal injury and loss following a road traffic collision. The claimants alleged that they were travelling in a BMW which was struck by the defendant's vehicle which allegedly failed to give way and drove into collision with the claimant's vehicle. The second defendant alleged that the claim was fraudulent. At first instance the county court held that the account given by the claimants was unsatisfactory and as such the claim failed. In a comment given in response to a request for clarification from counsel, the judge commented that:

> ***If it were necessary to do so, which it isn't, I would find that this was a fraudulent claim.***

The court of appeal set aside the first instance judge's findings of fraud when the court had approached the claim as needing a finding of either fraud or permitting the claim to succeed. Despite fraud having been pleaded, the claim can still fail without a finding of fraud being made, simply through the court finding that the claimant cannot prove their case to the necessary standard of proof.

In ***Rizan***, the court of appeal criticised the judge at first instance for making a finding of fraud and said that it was unnecessary as the claim could have been dismissed without a finding of fraud. The judge had not been faced with a binary choice between making a finding of fraud and finding for the claimants. The claimants had not satisfied the burden of proof, and the claim could be dismissed on that basis.

Court's approach at trial

The court has to decide what reliance it can place on the surveillance evidence, as discussed in chapter one, the weight that the court places on the evidence is a matter for the trial judge. By its nature, this is an issue that will vary depending upon the case that is in front of the court, and the surveillance footage that has been obtained. In this section three cases have been highlighted in order to demonstrate some of the potential approaches taken by the courts at trial after examining surveillance evidence.

The first case demonstrates how evidence and allegations made by a defendant are of such little assistance to the court, that they can have consequences for the defendant. In ***Kilbey v Arien Contractors Ltd [2019] Lexis Citation 470***, the claimant brought an action for damages for personal injuries against his former employers. Liability was admitted and the trial judge observed that the allegations of failure to mitigate loss and malingering should have been pleaded. The malingering allegation was not put until a counter-schedule was served on the 28 October 2019, approximately six weeks before trial. It was perhaps questionable as to whether the defendant ought to have raised the allegation of malingering because, the defendant's expert saw the surveillance evidence and said:

> ***that he did not believe that the claimant was exaggerating purposefully for gain.***

The judge observed:

> ***It seems to me that makes an allegation of malingering, the burden of which lies on the defendant, very difficult to sustain. In fact, it went further than that because none of the medical experts who had seen the claimant supported such a proposition.***
>
> ***In my judgment neither the social media nor the surveillance evidence has the value placed upon it by the defendants. I do not consider that either is incompatible with the claimant's general case.... The social media shots show that on occasion the claimant goes out (and has been abroad) and enjoys himself.***

> ***Again, I do not see that as incompatible with his case that he suffers pain and is not able to carry out manual work.***

The judge further stated:

> ***The defendant's counsel was critical of the claimant, both during cross-examination and in his final submissions. I have already said that there are grave difficulties in relation to the allegation of malingering properly so called, and having listened carefully to all the evidence I am satisfied that it is not only not made out but it should never have been advanced.***

As can be seen, evidence that does not address the pleaded case or is unsupported by the medico-legal evidence will be of little or no assistance to the court. In ***Kilbey***, the defendant's approach had consequences for them as the court ordered the defendant to pay indemnity costs from the day after the defendant made dishonesty allegations within the counter-schedule, as the evidence did not support the position that had been advanced.

The second case demonstrates how the claimant's case can be impacted by the surveillance evidence. In ***Hibberd-Little v Carlton [2018] EWHC 1787 (QB)***, The claimant brought an action for personal injury and losses arising from a road traffic collision and alleged that she had sustained life altering injuries because of the accident. The claimant valued her claim at close to £4.5m and alleged that she had had to give up a successful teaching career. Following the trial, the claimant was awarded £41,250. The claimant was awarded 25% of her costs until the date of the defendant's Part 36 offer, and ordered to pay the defendant's costs thereafter.

Whilst there were numerous factual findings made by the court, in relation to the surveillance evidence, the court found the claimant witness to be unsatisfactory when her responses were compared with the video surveillance. Interestingly, the claimant's own clear account contributed to her undoing. The court held:

> ***The obvious effort and levels of concentration required to complete her comprehensive review of the surveillance evidence***

> ***in her witness statement of 21 March 2018 speak eloquently of the claimant's capabilities, not least of all her memory and concentration.***

This does highlight a practical consideration for the claimant when preparing any response to the surveillance footage that they wish to serve, this issue was discussed in more detail in chapter four. The judgment highlights that the claimant needs to tread a careful line between explaining any inconsistencies and giving such a comprehensive response that they prove their own functional capabilities.

Lastly, the third case demonstrates how the court can consider the surveillance evidence and be satisfied that, whilst the allegations were properly advanced, the claimant has overcome the burden of proof to succeed in the claim. In ***Miley v Friends Life Ltd [2017] EWHC 2415 (QB)***, the claimant advanced a claim based upon her contention that she was suffering from chronic fatigue syndrome. The claimant's schedule of loss claimed significant on-going loss of earnings, the insurer alleged the claimant was exaggerating his symptoms.

The court reviewed the defendant's surveillance evidence and considered that the same was not unequivocal and the claimant was not seen doing anything that he said he could not do. Having heard the evidence and weighed the matters in consideration, the judge found that the claimant was believable and found the claimant's expert evidence more convincing. The court held that the surveillance evidence did not undermine the case presented and that the footage did not display anything of significance when considered against the statements of case relied upon. It is not unheard of to see cases where a large amount of stock is put into the weight of the surveillance evidence. The judgment in ***Miley*** is a cautionary reminder that surveillance is not always determinative of the issues in the case, and the overall effect of it on the pleaded case needs to be scrutinised.

Post-trial

After trial, some aggrieved defendants have continued to investigate cases where they consider the claim was fraudulent. This section examines how, if evidence is obtained through investigations post trial, the defendant can deploy that evidence and seek to rectify a potential fraud.

In ***Martin Raymond Owens v Mark Noble [2010] EWCA Civ 224***, the claimant was injured in an accident in September 2003. In March 2008, the high court awarded the claimant just over £3.3m in damages. A key component of the damages award was that the claimant had seriously impaired mobility, would never work again and would require substantial assistance with daily living. Later in 2008, the defendant's insurers received confidential information which cast doubt on the claimant's claims as to mobility, working capacity and requirement for living assistance.

The defendant appealed, out of time, and the court of appeal had to consider an application to set aside the high court judgment based on evidence that the claimant had deliberately misled the court as to his disabilities at trial. The recently acquired evidence, and the assertion that it showed a deliberate fraud, were in issue. The court had to consider whether the judgment was obtained by fraud or whether the claimant's displayed functional abilities were as a result of the successful outcome of post-trial therapy.

In considering the defendant's appeal, the court of appeal remitted the matter back to the trial judge, first to determine whether there had been a fraud, and then if so to re-assess the damages in light of the new evidence.

At the re-assessment of damages hearing, the court held that the claimant had not deliberately misled the court. The case establishes the important principle that, a case can be re-examined post-trial, although given the defendant did not succeed at the re-assessment hearing, this was something of a pyrrhic victory. It is however a reminder that even after trial a claimant can still be deprived of an award obtained through dishonest means.

This case has to be considered alongside that of ***Singh and others v Habib and another [2011] EWCA Civ 599***. In this case, three claimants brought claims for personal injury and losses arising from a road traffic collision. They alleged that a car driven by the first defendant failed to stop and collided with their stationary vehicle.

The first defendant did not co-operate with his insurers, who were the second defendants, and did not give evidence at trial. At trial, the district judge regarded two out of the three claimants to be unsatisfactory witnesses, he nevertheless found in favour of the claimants and awarded each of them damages. After judgment, the first defendant contacted his insurers' solicitors and gave a statement saying that the accident never took place. The first defendant also stated that he had been told by a woman associated with him that he had been promised £750 from each of the claimants for making a claim for an accident which never took place. It was also discovered that the first defendant's telephone number was the same as the telephone number of the claims company involved in the matter.

The insurers appealed and applied for permission to adduce this fresh evidence. The circuit judge refused the application, and the appeal was dismissed, the insurers appealed to the court of appeal who allowed the appeal and directed that the matter be re-heard by another circuit judge. The court of appeal held that the court would be particularly acute to consider questions of admitting fresh evidence as there is great public interest in the prevention of fraudulent road traffic claims. The *Ladd v Marshall* principles (discussed below) were not to be taken as a completely rigid framework and the public interest was sufficient to permit the fresh evidence. This was based on the premise that there was widespread concern about fraudulent road traffic claims, and that there was a strong public interest in a full investigation of all the evidence.

It is important to note that the court's judgment does not alter the fact that permitting new evidence on appeal should be rare, and that there is also a strong public interest in there being finality to litigation. Further, where fraud is alleged because of the new evidence, it will still be a question of judgment in every case whether the evidence is strong enough to justify a re-trial.

Where fresh evidence is adduced on appeal which may suggest that the judge at first instance was deliberately misled, the court will only allow the appeal and order a retrial where either the fraud is admitted or the evidence of it is incontrovertible. Where the fresh evidence amounts to an allegation of fraud which is contested, the usual course is to require the issue of fraud to be tried before the established judgment is set aside. However, it is not necessary to commence a fresh action to determine the fraud issue as we have seen from the authorities above. The trial of the fraud issue can and should be referred to a judge, pursuant to ***CPR 52.20(2)(b)*** which provides:

> **(2) The appeal court has power to—**
>
> > **(a) affirm, set aside or vary any order or judgment made or given by the lower court;**
> >
> > **(b) refer any claim or issue for determination by the lower court;**

Surveillance after judgment may disclose that the court was successfully misled as to the severity of the claimant's symptoms and disability. This may give rise to an appeal on principles set out in ***Ladd v Marshall [1954] 3 All ER 745*** which sets out that the court has to consider three points. These are:

> ***(1) the evidence could not have been obtained with reasonable diligence for use at the trial; (2) the evidence must be such that, if given, it would probably have an important influence on the result of the case, though it need not be decisive;***
>
> ***(3) the evidence must be such as is presumably to be believed; it must be apparently credible, though it need not be incontrovertible***

The more recent decision of ***Dale v Banga & Others [2021] EWCA Civ 240***, also provides assistance as to how the appellate court should approach the issue of the obtaining of evidence post trial which gives an indication that the judgment at first instance was obtained by fraud. The case concerned a dispute in relation to a number of wills. A will made in 2012, bequeathed the majority of the deceased's estate to the applicant. In 2013 a letter of revocation was made which revoked the 2012 will. The witnesses to the letter were the respondents. The letter of revocation was declared valid and since no other previous will was found to apply, the deceased was deemed to have died intestate.

Some considerable time went by before the applicant sought permission to appeal, and the appeal was brought on the basis that new evidence affected the credibility of the respondents and the validity of the letter of revocation. The new evidence was that one of the respondents had been convicted of fraudulent trading and money laundering, along with the first respondent's son. Furthermore, the evidence showed that the first respondent had also been involved with, and was accused of, attempting to pervert the course of justice through falsifying documents.

The court held that the new evidence did not meet the threshold required to succeed on appeal. The evidence did not relate to the facts of the case in hand and the criminal events took place after the letter of revocation was made. The new evidence challenged the credibility of the respondents, but this was a point that was considered during the original trial, and therefore was not enough to show that the letter of revocation was forged.

It can therefore be seen that, whilst it is possible to address judgments that have possibly been obtained by fraud after the trial has taken place, the threshold for the defendant to surmount is a high one.

CHAPTER SIX

COSTS CONSIDERATIONS

Surveillance evidence does not only impact upon the potential level of damages that a claimant may receive. Surveillance evidence can affect how the court approaches its order in relation to costs, both at an interlocutory stage and any final assessment hearing. It can lead to a party incurring costs liabilities and penalties, offers being re-evaluated and possibly accepted or withdrawn.

Costs budgets and costs and case management conferences

Whilst surveillance evidence is obtained in a range of cases, such evidence is usually obtained in multi-track cases, because in these cases the value of the claim is sufficient to justify the costs of obtaining the surveillance evidence. This does give rise to a practical concern because multi-track personal injury claims are usually subject to the rules in relation to costs budgets and often, but not always, subject to a Costs Management Order ('CMO'). *CPR 3.12(1)* provides:

> ***(1) This Section and Practice Direction 3E apply to all Part 7 multi-track cases, except—***
>
> > ***(a) where the claim is commenced on or after 22nd April 2014 and the amount of money claimed as stated on the claim form is £10 million or more; or***
> >
> > ***(b) where the claim is commenced on or after 22nd April 2014 and is for a monetary claim which is not quantified or not fully quantified or is for a non-monetary claim and in any such case the claim form contains a statement that the claim is valued at £10 million or more; or***
> >
> > ***(c) where in proceedings commenced on or after 6th April 2016 a claim is made by or on behalf of a person under the age of 18 (a child) (and on a child reaching majority***

> ***this exception will continue to apply unless the court otherwise orders); or***
>
> ***(d) where the proceeding are the subject of fixed costs or scale costs; or***
>
> ***(e) the court otherwise orders.***

As can be seen there are some cases that are exempt from the costs management process, but the majority of multi-track personal injury claims are subject to CMO's. In these cases, the court will consider how it can best manage costs and will often, but not always, hold a costs management hearing in order to manage the costs of the litigation. The purpose of costs management is set out at ***CPR 3.12(2)***:

> ***The purpose of costs management is that the court should manage both the steps to be taken and the costs to be incurred by the parties to any proceedings (or variation costs as provided in rule 3.15A) so as to further the overriding objective.***

The court's powers in controlling the costs of the litigation are set out at ***CPR 3.15***:

> ***(1) In addition to exercising its other powers, the court may manage the costs to be incurred (the budgeted costs) by any party in any proceedings.***
>
> ***(2) The court may at any time make a 'costs management order'. Where costs budgets have been filed and exchanged the court will make a costs management order unless it is satisfied that the litigation can be conducted justly and at proportionate cost in accordance with the overriding objective without such an order being made. By a costs management order the court will—***
>
> > ***(a) record the extent to which the budgeted costs are agreed between the parties;***
> >
> > ***(b) in respect of the budgeted costs which are not agreed, record the court's approval after making appropriate revisions;***

> ***(c) record the extent (if any) to which incurred costs are agreed.***

(3) If a costs management order has been made, the court will thereafter control the parties' budgets in respect of recoverable costs.

In conducting a costs budget exercise, the court is noting the costs that have been spent, and reviewing the costs that are being proposed to be spent, in order to ensure that the costs expended on the case are reasonable and proportionate. In the vast majority of multi-track personal injury cases, the court will make a CMO, usually, these orders are made at the time when the court makes its directions order at the outset of the litigation. In order to manage the costs of the litigation, the court has to know what costs the parties are proposing to incur. How then does the court address the issue concerning the costs of surveillance evidence? As will be seen below, pursuant to ***CPR 44.4.(3)(h)***, when deciding the amount of costs, the court has to have regard to:

the receiving party's last approved or agreed budget.

This causes a difficulty for the court, as it cannot have regard to a costs budget that did not contain the costs of the surveillance evidence. If the costs of the surveillance evidence are outlined in the costs budget, then the element of surprise is lost, and the claimant will be aware of the presence of the evidence. On a strict reading of the CPR the party obtaining the surveillance evidence either has to reference its existence, or potentially forfeit any ability to recover the costs of it. How then is the court to control the costs of the litigation and ensure that the element of surprise is not denied to the party obtaining the surveillance evidence?

The high court addressed the position in the case of ***Purser (Gemma) v Hibbs (Robert) & Anr [2015] EWHC 1792 (QB)***. Part of the court's judgment related to the effect the surveillance evidence had on a part 36 offer made by the defendant, and this issue is addressed in more detail in the part 36 section below.

By way of background, the claimant brought a claim for personal injury and losses following a road traffic accident. Liability was admitted and expert evidence was prepared. The defendant's insurers decided to conduct surveillance and in August 2013 made a part 36 offer of £95,000. The claimant did not originally accept the offer but did subsequently accept it when the defendant disclosed the surveillance evidence in October 2014.

In considering the costs of the surveillance evidence, the court was satisfied that the facts of the case showed that the surveillance was reasonably conducted and did disclose deceit on the part of the claimant. The evidence demonstrated a good reason for allowing the costs of the surveillance evidence and for doing so despite the fact that the matters were not referred to at any time in the cost budgets. The court expressly stated that it would not wish to discourage the judicious use of surveillance evidence or alert fraudsters to the use of surveillance evidence, the court stated:

> ***The status of surveillance evidence is anomalous in relation to the costs case management and costs budgeting rules. Those rules do not make any express provision for what we are to do about the costs of surveillance evidence. They are obviously a special case. Most litigation is conducted on a "cards on the table" basis, and the costs budgeting system provides for each side to declare to the other in advance and to declare to the court what it proposes to spend so that the cost budgeting process can take place. Of course, some degree of cunning is required in the administration of surveillance, for entirely legitimate and understandable reasons, particularly given the appalling level of insurance fraud of which the judges become increasingly aware the longer they sit in that field. The court would not, I think, wish to do anything to discourage the judicious use of surveillance evidence or to alert actual or prospective fraudsters to the likelihood of it…I do not consider it sits in the mouth of a fraudulent or deceitful Claimant to object to paying for the reasonable costs of the very work that has exposed their deceit, let alone to object on so technical and undeserving a basis as reliance on cost budgeting.***

Prior to the high court's judgment, there had been differing opinions as to how the costs of surveillance evidence should be approached in costs budgets. Some courts had questioned how a statement of truth on a costs budget can be signed when it is known that a revision will need to be made when surveillance evidence is served. In contrast to this, others have queried how a defendant can reasonably keep hold of crucial evidence that needs to be disclosed at a tactical point in the case if they are required to disclose its existence for administrative reasons at an interlocutory stage.

Until this judgment, the issue of how to approach surveillance evidence in costs budgets had been a relevant issue for defendants to consider for some time, as the concept of keeping part of your case secret is anomalous with the prospective approach of costs budgets. It is impossible to maintain the necessary secrecy over surveillance evidence if the costs associated with it have to be disclosed at a CCMC, which will take place before directions regarding disclosure and witness evidence have been complied with.

The court's decision in ***Purser*** supports the defendant's position that surveillance evidence still needs to be kept secret for the purposes of costs budgets and the court gave a specific endorsement that it does not want to hinder the judicious use of such evidence. A defendant can always include the costs of surveillance evidence in their costs budget, but this would cause the required element of secrecy to be lost.

The court's approach helpfully indicates that this secrecy surrounding surveillance evidence does not invalidate the recoverability of the costs. In order to succeed in recovering those costs though the court will need to examine the overall position of the case including the cogency of the surveillance evidence, its effect upon the case and how the claimant's claim has been advanced.

Court's costs powers

Should the surveillance evidence have such an impact on the case that the court sanctions a party in costs, when approaching the issue of costs, it has to be remembered that the court has a wide discretion. Both at an interlocutory stage and the final trial the court can exercise wide powers to determine where the costs of the litigation lie and what order it considers appropriate to make. ***CPR 44.2*** provides:

(1) The court has discretion as to –

(a) whether costs are payable by one party to another;

(b) the amount of those costs; and

(c) when they are to be paid.

(2) If the court decides to make an order about costs –

(a) the general rule is that the unsuccessful party will be ordered to pay the costs of the successful party; but

(b) the court may make a different order.

...

(4) In deciding what order (if any) to make about costs, the court will have regard to all the circumstances, including

(a) the conduct of all the parties;

(b) whether a party has succeeded on part of its case, even if that party has not been wholly successful; and

(c) any admissible offer to settle made by a party which is drawn to the court's attention, and which is not an offer to which costs consequences under Part 36 apply.

(5) The conduct of the parties includes –

(a) conduct before, as well as during, the proceedings and in particular the extent to which the parties followed the Practice Direction – Pre-Action Conduct or any relevant pre-action protocol;

(b) whether it was reasonable for a party to raise, pursue or contest a particular allegation or issue;

(c) the manner in which a party has pursued or defended its case or a particular allegation or issue; and

(d) whether a claimant who has succeeded in the claim, in whole or in part, exaggerated its claim.

(6) The orders which the court may make under this rule include an order that a party must pay –

(a) a proportion of another party's costs;

(b) a stated amount in respect of another party's costs;

(c) costs from or until a certain date only;

(d) costs incurred before proceedings have begun;

(e) costs relating to particular steps taken in the proceedings;

(f) costs relating only to a distinct part of the proceedings; and

(g) interest on costs from or until a certain date, including a date before judgment.

As can be seen, the court's powers are extensive, the court can make a variety of costs orders, and each case will turn on its own facts. When exercising its discretion under *CPR 44.2*, the court will have regard to *CPR 44.4* which provides:

(1) The court will have regard to all the circumstances in deciding whether costs were –

(a) if it is assessing costs on the standard basis –

(i) proportionately and reasonably incurred; or

(ii) proportionate and reasonable in amount, or

(b) if it is assessing costs on the indemnity basis –

(i) unreasonably incurred; or

(ii) unreasonable in amount.

(2) In particular, the court will give effect to any orders which have already been made.

(3) The court will also have regard to –

(a) the conduct of all the parties, including in particular –

(i) conduct before, as well as during, the proceedings; and

(ii) the efforts made, if any, before and during the proceedings in order to try to resolve the dispute;

(b) the amount or value of any money or property involved;

(c) the importance of the matter to all the parties;

(d) the particular complexity of the matter or the difficulty or novelty of the questions raised;

(e) the skill, effort, specialised knowledge and responsibility involved;

(f) the time spent on the case;

(g) the place where and the circumstances in which work or any part of it was done; and

(h) the receiving party's last approved or agreed budget.

It can therefore be seen that the court firstly has a discretion as to whether a costs order is made or not, in some cases the court has marked its displeasure as to how a case has been brought or defended, by depriving a litigant of their costs, awarding them a percentage of their costs, or awarding them on the indemnity basis. A full examination of the case law in relation to the court's approach as to what costs orders are made in particular circumstances is beyond the remit of this text, and a list of examples would be extensive. The general principle is examined below with a view to how surveillance evidence can impact upon the award for costs.

As can be seen, the court has to take numerous factors into account when deciding what the appropriate costs order is to make. The court has to weigh the nature of the case, the balance of the evidence presented and the conduct of the parties, to reach the appropriate order. In cases where the defendant's surveillance evidence has reduced the claimant's claim by a significant amount the courts have been willing to penalise the claimant in costs. As set out above, the case law in this regard is extensive, but of note is the case of ***Marcus v Medway Primary Care Trust [2011] EWCA Civ 750***, where the claimant recovered £2,000 on a claim for £525,000, the court of appeal held that the defendants were the winners and awarded them 75% of their costs. When approaching the issue of whether to make an alternative award for costs, the court has to examine whether any exaggeration had a causative effect upon the claim, and whether this caused any costs to be incurred or wasted.

It should be noted though that, whilst the courts can and do have the power to make such costs orders, it does not follow that, just because the defendant has reduced the level of damages awarded by a significant amount against what was claimed, that the court will always exercise its powers. The causative effect of any exaggeration on the issue of costs is the key factor.

Qualified on way costs shifting

Qualified one-way costs shifting ('QOCS') was introduced in April 2013 as part of the more widespread 'Jackson Reforms' that were implemented to reduce costs and delay in the civil justice system. The QOCS rules mean that a claimant who is unsuccessful in their claim does not have to pay the defendant's costs of defending the claim except in limited circumstances, which will be discussed later in this section.

QOCS only applies to claims for personal injury, it was established in the case of ***Faiz Siddiqui v The Chancellor, Masters and Scholars of The University of Oxford*** [2018] ***EWHC 536 (QB)*** that where a claim is pursued for something other than, or in addition to personal injury such as pure financial loss, QOCS will not apply.

The CPR sets out the relevant rule in relation to QOCS and ***CPR 44.13-16*** inclusive provides:

> ***(1) This Section applies to proceedings which include a claim for damages –***
>
> > ***(a) for personal injuries;***
> >
> > ***(b) under the Fatal Accidents Act 1976; or***
> >
> > ***(c) which arises out of death or personal injury and survives for the benefit of an estate by virtue of section 1(1) of the Law Reform (Miscellaneous Provisions) Act 1934,***
> >
> > ***but does not apply to applications pursuant to section 33 of the Senior Courts Act 1981 or section 52 of the County Courts Act 1984 (applications for pre-action disclosure), or where rule 44.17 applies.***
>
> ***(2) In this Section, 'claimant' means a person bringing a claim to which this Section applies or an estate on behalf of which such a claim is brought, and includes a person making a counterclaim or an additional claim.***
>
> ***Effect of qualified one-way costs shifting***
>
> ***44.14***
>
> ***(1) Subject to rules 44.15 and 44.16, orders for costs made against a claimant may be enforced without the permission of the court but only to the extent that the aggregate amount in money terms of such orders does not exceed the aggregate amount in money terms of any orders for damages and interest made in favour of the claimant.***

(2) Orders for costs made against a claimant may only be enforced after the proceedings have been concluded and the costs have been assessed or agreed.

(3) An order for costs which is enforced only to the extent permitted by paragraph (1) shall not be treated as an unsatisfied or outstanding judgment for the purposes of any court record.

Exceptions to qualified one-way costs shifting where permission not required

44.15 Orders for costs made against the claimant may be enforced to the full extent of such orders without the permission of the court where the proceedings have been struck out on the grounds that –

> *(a) the claimant has disclosed no reasonable grounds for bringing the proceedings;*
>
> *(b) the proceedings are an abuse of the court's process; or*
>
> *(c) the conduct of –*
>
> > *(i) the claimant; or*
> >
> > *(ii) a person acting on the claimant's behalf and with the claimant's knowledge of such conduct, is likely to obstruct the just disposal of the proceedings.*

Exceptions to qualified one-way costs shifting where permission required

44.16

(1) Orders for costs made against the claimant may be enforced to the full extent of such orders with the permission of the court where the claim is found on the balance of probabilities to be fundamentally dishonest.

> ***(2) Orders for costs made against the claimant may be enforced up to the full extent of such orders with the permission of the court, and to the extent that it considers just, where –***
>
> > ***(a) the proceedings include a claim which is made for the financial benefit of a person other than the claimant or a dependant within the meaning of section 1(3) of the Fatal Accidents Act 1976 (other than a claim in respect of the gratuitous provision of care, earnings paid by an employer or medical expenses); or***
> >
> > ***(b) a claim is made for the benefit of the claimant other than a claim to which this Section applies.***
>
> ***(3) Where paragraph (2)(a) applies, the court may, subject to rule 46.2, make an order for costs against a person, other than the claimant, for whose financial benefit the whole or part of the claim was made.***

The court can remove the claimant's QOCS protection in circumstances where the claim is fundamentally dishonest, where it is struck out as an abuse of process or obstructs the just disposal of proceedings. Issues of fundamental dishonesty and abuse of process are examined in chapter seven. It is noteworthy at this stage though to recognise that, surveillance evidence that completely undermines the fabric of the claim can lead to a claimant losing QOCS protection if the court considers the claimant's actions are so egregiously dishonest.

As we have seen in the costs sections examined above, when assessing costs the court has to look at the causative effect of any exaggeration in a claim. A claimant who has advanced a claim that may have some degree of exaggeration will not automatically lose their QOCS protection. The court has to examine the effect of that exaggeration and whether it taints the claim to such a degree that it is a fundamentally dishonest claim.

Effect on settlement offers

As discussed above, the case of ***Purser (Gemma) v Hibbs (Robert) & Anr [2015] EWHC 1792 (QB)*** had a wider effect outside of the rule that it established in respect of how surveillance evidence is treated for the purposes of costs budgeting. As will be recalled, the claimant had brought a claim for personal injury and losses following a road traffic accident. Liability was admitted and expert evidence was prepared. The defendant's insurers decided to conduct surveillance, and in August 2013 made a part 36 offer of £95,000.

The claimant did not originally accept the offer but did subsequently accept it when the defendant disclosed the surveillance evidence in October 2014. It was common ground that the defendant was entitled to its costs following expiry of the part 36 offer. The issue before the court was whether the claimant should be entitled to its costs up to that date. This fell to be decided under the pre-April 2015 rules and according to CPR r.36.10(5) under which the normal costs consequences apply "unless the court orders otherwise".

The defendant argued that as the claim was dishonest and was exaggerated, that he should be allowed his costs both before and after the date of expiry of the offer. His Honour Judge Moloney QC held that although the old rule 36.10 gives no express guidance as to the criteria to be applied, a test was set out in the case of ***Lumb v Hampsey (2011) EWHC 2808 (QB)***. That test appears to be indistinguishable from the new ***CPR r.36.13(5)*** so that the appropriate test is whether the usual costs rules should be departed from because it would be unjust to apply them. In considering this, the court had in mind that the claimant had been malingering and was capable of working and caring for herself. The claimant had been misleading lawyers and medical experts as far back as when the part 36 offer was made.

The defendant however could not establish that the claimant's deceitful conduct extended back before the time they made the part 36 offer and as such could not show that it was unjust to depart from the normal costs rule.

The court had other powers to utilise against the claimant, and it was appropriate to stigmatise the claimant's conduct by directing that the defendant's costs from the date of expiry of the part 36 offer should be paid on the indemnity basis along with interest. It was also appropriate to order that the claimant pay the costs of the surveillance evidence on the indemnity basis even though such costs were not included in the cost budgets.

The court's decision regarding the costs consequences of part 36 highlights the broad range of powers the court has to determine costs. As ever though costs remain a case sensitive point where the court has a wide discretion when deciding what order is appropriate in each case.

Even though the claimant was deceitful and was caught out by the surveillance evidence, it was not unjust to depart from the normal costs rule as the defendant could not overcome the hurdle that the claimant's conduct extended back beyond the part 36 offer and as such could not satisfy the court that it was appropriate to depart from the normal rule. The judgment therefore reinforces the approach by the courts that there should not be frequent deviation from normal rules as this might create uncertainty.

The judgment in ***Purser*** has to be viewed in conjunction with the case of ***Yvonne Hazel Painting v University of Oxford [2005] EWCA Civ 161***, where the claimant had been found to have intentionally exaggerated her claim. Based upon this exaggeration, the defendant could be viewed to have been the overall winning party despite having its payment into court beaten. The defendant was therefore entitled to its costs since the court was bound to take into account the conduct of the parties and the absence by the claimant of any intention to settle the matter.

As was discussed at the outset of this chapter, the court has a wide discretion when addressing costs and pursuant to ***CPR 44.3(4)(a)*** & ***(5)(d)***, the court has to have regard to the conduct of the parties and also to whether a claim has been exaggerated. This can impact upon both the assessment of costs and where those costs lie. This is a very fact specific exercise, and the court of appeal held in ***Morgan v UPS [2008] EWCA Civ 1476***, that the court has to have regard for the broader picture in the case when determining the costs liabilities after findings of fact have been made.

Defendants should not take it for granted though that following ***Painting***, courts will award them costs protection as of right in the face of good quality surveillance evidence. The court noted in ***Russell Adrian***

Knibbs v (1) Heart of England NHS Foundation Trust (2) Dr G Koshy (3) Dr P Mehta [2017] Lexis Citation 311, that a defendant who has obtained surveillance evidence can protect itself with a modest part 36 offer. An attempt by the defendant to suggest that they should have costs protection if their part 36 offer is beaten by the claimant may not be met with much enthusiasm by the court.

Defendants have a range of settlement methods open to them and making a Calderbank offer is an alternative method of trying to settle the claim. Calderbank offers have been permissible in civil litigation since the case of ***Calderbank v Calderbank [1975] 3 All ER 333 (EWCA)***. This case introduced the concept of a settlement offer being made 'without prejudice save as to costs', this means that if the offer is not accepted, it cannot be referred to during the course of the proceedings, but it can be referred to the court on the question of costs. This section is not designed to discuss the pros and cons of making a Calderbank offer as opposed to a part 36 offer, but Calderbank offers may be used as an alternative to part 36 offers. If an Offeror is making a part 36 offer, then they must comply with the strict requirements of part 36 of the CPR, there is no corresponding rule by which an Offeror making a Calderbank offer must comply. Calderbank offers therefore permit a greater degree of flexibility than part 36 offers, for example, a Calderbank offer can vary issues such as the time period for which the offer is open and the timescales for payment, and this can have advantages in certain situations.

In cases where the defendant takes the position that the claim is fraudulent, a Calderbank offer can afford the defendant the flexibility to offer to settle any genuine aspect of the claim and costs associated with that aspect of the claim, but not offer to settle the fraudulent aspect of the claim.

Whilst a Calderbank offer provides greater flexibility in how the offer can be termed, the costs consequences that flow from such an offer are not as well prescribed as those which flow from a well-placed part 36 offer, and are very much at the discretion of the court. The costs consequences that flow from a well-pitched part 36 offer are strict.

Revising offers

A party may feel that the surveillance evidence it has disclosed is likely to have such an effect on their opponent's case that they can revisit and either withdraw or change a part 36 offer which has been made previously. These are very tactical considerations which need to be taken after careful examination of the evidence and position. A party taking rash action could find itself withdrawing or changing the terms of its part 36 offer only to find it has lost the costs protection it had built up. In these cases, ***CPR 36.9&10*** will need to be considered, it should be noted that this section only applies to part 36 offers and not to other types of settlement offer.

The starting point is to consider ***CPR 36.9(1)***, this states that the terms of a part 36 offer can only be changed if the Offeree has not accepted the part 36 offer. If the part 36 offer has not been accepted, then a notice withdrawing or changing the terms of the offer must served on the Offeree. Readers will note the reference to 'service' and parties should consider ***CPR 6.26*** in relation to service of such notices and when they are deemed to be served.

The next consideration is when was the part 36 offer made? In order to be valid, pursuant to ***CPR 36.5(1) (c)***, a part 36 offer must specify a period of not less than 21 days within which the defendant will be liable for the claimant's costs if the offer is accepted, this time frame is referred to as the 'Relevant Period'. If the Relevant Period has not expired, then ***CPR 36.10*** applies and the Offeree can serve a notice of acceptance of the part 36 offer of the original part 36 offer, as long as they do so prior to the expiration of the Relevant Period.

If this happens, then, pursuant to ***CPR 36.10(2)(b)***, the Offeror has seven days from the Offeree's notice of acceptance to apply to court to withdraw or change the terms of the offer. When dealing with the application, the court may give permission for the original part 36 offer to be withdrawn or its terms changed, if satisfied that there has been a change of circumstances since the making of the original part 36 offer, and that it is in the interests of justice to give permission.

In ***Jayne Ellen Evans v Royal Wolverhampton Hospitals NHS Foundation Trust [2014] EWHC 3185 (QB)***, the court held that the test to be applied when the court is considering whether to give a party permission to withdraw a part 36 offer is whether there has been a sufficient change of circumstances to make it just to permit the party to withdraw its offer. Such examples would include:

> ***the discovery of further evidence which puts a wholly different complexion on the case ... or a change in the legal outlook brought about by a new judicial decision...***

If the Relevant Period has expired, then ***CPR 36.9(4)*** allows the Offeror to withdraw or change the terms of a part 36 offer without the permission of the court. The question for the parties is then what effect that revised part 36 offer has on costs. ***CPR 36.9(5)*** provides:

> ***Where the offeror changes the terms of a Part 36 offer to make it more advantageous to the offeree:***
>
> ***(a) such improved offer shall be treated, not as the withdrawal of the original offer; but as the making of a new Part 36 offer on the improved terms;***

There is no specific rule that states that the revision of an offer downwards by a defendant will not be treated as a new offer, but is left open to implication by the wording of the rules. The county court, in the non-binding decision of ***Amy Elizabeth Burrett v Mencap Limited [2014]***, found that where the defendant had varied a part 36 offer to make it less advantageous to the claimant, the time that is given in that original offer is the time that applies. The claimant was not entitled to another 21-day period in which to consider the part 36 offer, and the defendant retained the costs protection from the date of the original part 36 offer.

CHAPTER SEVEN

FURTHER ACTIONS

In more egregious cases, the effect of surveillance evidence can lead to findings being made by the court that can have repercussions for a litigant's future after the court has handed down its judgment. These implications can come in the form of costs, as seen in chapter six, and in further action being taken against a litigant who has advanced a claim on a false basis. As set out previously, it does not follow that surveillance evidence will always fundamentally undermine the fabric of a claim. Depending on the severity of any false statements of truth, surveillance evidence can form the basis for proceedings for contempt of court or even criminal action being brought.

This book is not intended to be an in-depth analysis of all of the options available when a court makes a finding that a claim has been brought on a false basis. This chapter is intended to outline two important consequences that can arise, these being findings of fundamental dishonesty and contempt of court proceedings.

Evidence to support findings of fundamental dishonesty and proceedings for contempt of court (discussed in more detail below), is not just found in surveillance footage. The evidence can come from a wide range of sources including social media, witness evidence and medical evidence to name but a few, and these issues are outside the remit of this text. With the purpose of this book being to focus on surveillance evidence, the topics below are discussed on the basis that any evidence used to support these contentions is based upon surveillance footage.

Fundamental dishonesty

Exaggeration in claims is not unknown, not all exaggeration is conscious or fatal to a claim. Some exaggeration by a claimant may be natural and understandable, some claimants will wish to impress upon their medico-legal experts and lawyers how their injuries have affected their lives so as to not underestimate a genuine condition, this can sometimes lead to a perhaps subconscious exaggeration. Conversely, the courts cannot tolerate the advancing of claims that are based on conscious exaggeration and dishonesty. It is clearly in the public interest that personal injury claimants pursue honest claims before the courts, but that they do not significantly exaggerate those claims for financial gain. How though do the courts address cases which are not wholly honest, but not grossly exaggerated? In ***Widlake v BAA Ltd [2009] EWCA Civ 1256***, Ward LJ stated:

> ***lies are told in litigation every day up and down the country and quite rightly do not lead to a penalty being imposed… there is a considerable difference between a concocted claim and an exaggerated claim.***

If a claim is fundamentally dishonest, then the court has a variety of powers to address the issues. An early example of the court's powers was set out in the case of ***Fairclough Homes Ltd v Summers [2012] UKSC 26***. In this case Mr Summers suffered a fracture to his ankle in an accident on a building site. The claimant brought a claim for damages, at one stage valued in excess of £800,000. At first instance, the claim for damages was found to be fraudulent, it should be noted that this finding was not just based upon surveillance evidence but a wide range of evidence that was disclosed in order to build a cumulative defence position.

The supreme court held that to deliberately make a false claim, and to serve false evidence is an abuse of process. The court has the power to strike out such a case under ***CPR 3.4(2)(b)***, which provides:

> ***(2) The court may strike out a statement of case if it appears to the court –***
>
> > ***(b) that the statement of case is an abuse of the court's process or is otherwise likely to obstruct the just disposal of the proceedings;***

The supreme court held that this power can be exercised at any time in proceedings, this includes at the end of trial, although this power would only be exercised in exceptional circumstances. Therefore, the court can strike out a claim if it is fraudulent, and whether a claim is an abuse of process on these grounds will depend upon the facts of each case. An example of the court exercising this power, and the factors examined, can be seen in the case of ***Victoria Admans v Two Saints Ltd [2016] 6 WLUK 611***, in the county court sitting in Swindon, where the judge found that a personal injury claim should be struck out prior to trial as an abuse of process. This was based on the claimant's dishonest exaggeration of her disability, which had been maintained over an extended period of time. The duration of time over which the dishonesty had been maintained and the exaggeration of the medical condition, tainted the whole of her claim.

When considering whether to strike out the claim, the court will examine such features as how long a period of time the exaggeration was conducted, what aspects of the claim it affected and whether the exaggeration was dishonest. As was seen in chapter six, if the court considers that a claim is an abuse of process then the claimant may be deprived of QOCS protection.

The provision for further action to be taken following the disclosure of surveillance evidence depends on the facts of the case. This is exemplified in the judgment of ***Karapetianas v Kent and Sussex Loft Conversions Ltd [2017] EWHC 859 (QB)***, where it was held that whilst the high court found a significant discrepancy between a claimant's presentation in covert surveillance evidence with that of the medico-legal evidence in a personal injury claim, the court declined to strike out the claim for abuse of process.

The ability to strike out a claim under ***CPR 3.4(2)(b)*** is not the only power the court has to address fraudulent claims. The court has the power pursuant to the ***Criminal Justice and Courts Act (2015)*** to dismiss a personal injury claim which is fundamentally dishonest, unless the court is satisfied that the claimant would suffer substantial injustice. This only applies to claims where the claim form was issued after 13 April 2015 and applies where, on the balance of probabilities the claim, or a related claim, has been brought on a fundamentally dishonest basis. ***s57 Criminal Justice and Courts Act*** provides:

> *(1) This section applies where, in proceedings on a claim for damages in respect of personal injury ("the primary claim")—*
>
> *(a) the court finds that the claimant is entitled to damages in respect of the claim, but*
>
> *(b) on an application by the defendant for the dismissal of the claim under this section, the court is satisfied on the balance of probabilities that the claimant has been fundamentally dishonest in relation to the primary claim or a related claim.*
>
> *(2) The court must dismiss the primary claim, unless it is satisfied that the claimant would suffer substantial injustice if the claim were dismissed.*

In order to examine this issue, the concept is broken down in the next two sections to examine what is 'fundamental' and what is 'dishonest'.

Fundamental

An early judgment as to the definition of fundamental dishonesty came from HHJ Moloney QC in the county court sitting in Cambridge, in the case of ***Michael Gosling v (1) Hailo & (2) Screwfix Direct [2014] Lexis Citation 316***. In this case the court stated at paragraphs 44 and 45 of the judgment:

> ***It appears to me that this phrase in the rules has to be interpreted purposively and contextually in the light of the context. This is, of course, the determination of whether the claimant is "deserving", as Jackson LJ put it, of the protection (from the costs liability that would otherwise fall on him) extended, for reasons of social policy, by the QOCS rules. It appears to me that when one looks at the matter in that way, one sees that what the rules are doing is distinguishing between two levels of dishonesty: dishonesty in relation to the claim which is not fundamental so as to expose such a claimant to costs liability, and dishonesty which is fundamental, so as to give rise to costs liability.***

> ***The corollary term to "fundamental" would be a word with some such meaning as "incidental" or "collateral". Thus, a claimant should not be exposed to costs liability merely because he is shown to have been dishonest as to some collateral matter or perhaps as to some minor, self-contained head of damage. If, on the other hand, the dishonesty went to the root of either the whole of his claim or a substantial part of his claim, then it appears to me that it would be a fundamentally dishonest claim: a claim which depended as to a substantial or important part of itself upon dishonesty.***

Subsequently, the court of appeal endorsed this definition in the case of ***Howlett v Davies [2017] EWHC Civ 1696.*** This supports the comments of Ward LJ in recognising that a degree of exaggeration does not automatically lead to the most severe of consequences being imposed upon a claimant. The issue for the court to examine is whether or not the very essence of the claim is fundamentally dishonest. In these circumstances the court may choose to exercise its powers to dismiss the claim and deprive the claimant of QOCS protection.

The approach taken in ***Howlett*** can be seen in the case of ***Tess Garraway v Holland & Barrett Ltd [2020] 3 WLUK 582***, where the county court sitting at Brighton held that:

> ***the claimant's personal injury claim against the defendant retailer would be dismissed, as she had been fundamentally dishonest in the presentation of her case relating to her main alleged injury.***

The court of appeal's judgment in ***Howlett*** also establishes the important principle that the defendant does not have to plead fundamental dishonesty in a statement of case. As was discussed in chapter five, it cannot be the case though that defendants can simply ambush the claimant with the issue, claimants must be given an adequate warning of, and a proper opportunity to deal with the point. Frequently this takes place when at trial, during cross-examination, an allegation of dishonesty is put to a claimant so that it can be explored during the claimant's evidence.

The judgment in ***Howlett*** is also helpful when considering how fundamental dishonesty that has not been pleaded in a statement of case should be addressed at trial. The court stated at paragraph 39 of its judgment:

> ***It is perhaps worth adding two comments. First, where a witness' honesty is to be challenged, it will always be best if that is explicitly put to the witness. There can then be no doubt that honesty is in issue. But what ultimately matters is that the witness has had fair notice of a challenge to his or her honesty and an opportunity to deal with it. It may be that in a particular context a cross-examination which does not use the words "dishonest" or "lying" will give a witness fair warning. That will be a matter for the trial judge to decide. Secondly, the fact that a party has not alleged fraud in his pleading may not preclude him from suggesting to a witness in cross-examination that he is lying. That must, in fact, be a common occurrence.***

The key point for the defendant in advancing the issue is, to ensure that it is put to the witness otherwise submissions cannot be made on the point at the end of the trial.

Dishonesty

The above section looks at how the courts approach the issue of what is categorised as being 'fundamental' in the test of fundamental dishonesty. This section examines what is classed as 'dishonest' in the test. The test for dishonesty is set out in the case of ***Ivey v Genting Casinos (UK) Ltd [2017] UKSC 67***. The case does not arise from a personal injury claim but a claim for unpaid gambling winnings. The claimant was a professional poker player. He visited one of the defendant's premises and played and won a series of games of Punto Banco. The winnings totalled £7.7m, the defendant did not pay out these monies as they believed the claimant had cheated by using an 'edge sorting' technique to gain an unfair advantage. The claimant sued the defendant to recover his winnings.

The parties agreed that there was an implied term between the gambler and the casino that forbade cheating. The supreme court held that the claimant had cheated, and accordingly he was not entitled to the winnings, and held the fact-finding tribunal must conduct a two-stage exercise. First the court must subjectively ascertain the actual state of the individual's knowledge or belief as to the facts, secondly the court must then determine whether the individual's conduct was honest or dishonest by the objective standards of ordinary decent people. There is no requirement that the defendant must appreciate that what he has done is, by those standards, dishonest.

When assessing if a personal injury claim is fundamentally dishonest, the high court held in ***London Organising Committee of the Olympic and Paralympic Games v Sinfield [2018] EWHC 51 (QB)*** that:

> ***a claimant should be found to be fundamentally dishonest within the meaning of s 57(1)(b) if the defendant proves on a balance of probabilities that the claimant has acted dishonestly in relation to the primary claim and/or a related claim (as defined in s 57(8)), and that he has thus substantially affected the presentation of his case, either in respects of liability or quantum, in a way which potentially adversely affected the defendant in a significant way, judged in the context of the particular facts and circumstances of the litigation. Dishonesty is to be judged according to the test set out by the Supreme Court in Ivey v Genting Casinos Limited***

In this case the claimant had advanced a genuine claim for an injury sustained whilst volunteering at the London Olympic Games. Part of the claim for special damages comprised alleged expenditure on gardening services, which were supported by invoices. These invoices though had not been issued by the gardener who the claimant said he had retained to provide the services. This was a substantial element of the claim for damages and as it was supported by false invoices, the claim stood to be struck out because of the claimant's dishonesty in relying upon the false invoices to support a head of loss claimed.

The nature of this remedy though needs to be carefully considered, in ***Spencer Smith v Ashwell Maintenance Ltd [2019] 1 WLUK 541***, the county court was satisfied that the claimant had not engaged in fundamentally dishonest conduct and held that:

> ***A gas engineer was entitled to damages from his employer for an ankle injury sustained after falling into a hole at work. Although there had been a degree of overstatement of his pain and its effect on him, the claimant had not been fundamentally dishonest. He had merely engaged in such conduct in order to convince, rather than deceive, medical experts as to his injury following the employer's vigorous attempts to avoid fully compensating him.***

In the case of ***Sudhirkumar Patel v (1) Arriva Midlands Ltd (2) Zurich Insurance PLC [2019] EWHC 1216 (QB)***, the high court struck out a personal injury claim as:

> ***being fundamentally dishonest where the claimant, who had been injured in a road collision, had presented to the neurological experts instructed in the claim as unable to move or communicate, but surveillance evidence showed him walking and talking.***

What can be taken from the above line of authorities, is that overstatement of a claim is not enough to be categorised as fundamentally dishonest. The claimant must engage in conduct that is dishonest when considered against the standards of ordinary decent people and which affects a central issue or issues in the claim.

Timing

In ***Patel v Arriva Midlands Ltd and another [2019] EWHC 1216 (QB)***, the court held that an application to dismiss a personal injury claim because of fundamental dishonesty could be determined at any time after the claimant's entitlement to damages is established. The court has the power to determine such an application before a quantum trial, but whether it should or not will depend on whether it can be determined justly at that time. This will be assessed on a case-by-case basis, because whilst the court could only find fundamental dishonesty once it had first found that the claimant was entitled to damages, the legislation did not provide that the court must first carry out a quantum assessment of the full claim before fundamental dishonesty could be found.

It should be remembered that the court does not have to either allow the claim or find fundamental dishonesty. In ***Wright v Satellite Information [2018] EWHC 812 (QB)***, the court found:

> ***It was the defendant's case that surveillance evidence had shown that the claimant was far less disabled than he claimed but nonetheless the claimant had been broadly consistent in what he had said in relation to the need for ongoing assistance. The rejection of the care claim was found to have flowed from a proper analysis of what was actually being done for the claimant and the conclusion that it did not properly sound in damages because "it was almost impossible... to value such occasional assistance". That was not the same as dishonesty. The trial judge was entitled to make findings of fact that he did and interpret the evidence as he did.***

As can be seen the court is not faced with a binary concept, the court can still find that the claimant has not proved their claim, but that the defendant has not established that the claimant has been fundamentally dishonest.

Contempt proceedings

It should be noted that, whilst this section on contempt proceedings follows the section on fundamental dishonesty, there is no rule or precedent to support a contention that, just because a person has been found to be fundamentally dishonest, that they are guilty of a contempt of court. The two issues are determined on different principles, and in some cases, are tried by different courts. The reader should not assume that just because a finding of fundamental dishonesty has been made in a case, that proceedings for contempt of court are either justified, or will succeed.

This text is not intended to be an in-depth analysis of contempt of court proceedings. For those parties who do deploy surveillance evidence, the consideration can and does arise as to whether further action in the form of proceedings for contempt of court, ought to be brought. This is an area where the party contemplating such action needs to proceed with caution, and the most careful consideration needs to be given as to whether such proceedings are justified and can substantiated. As is examined below, the penalties for contempt of court can be significant. Exercising these powers is not something that a court will take lightly, and consequently any contempt must be proved to the criminal standard of proof, ie. beyond reasonable doubt.

Proceedings for contempt of court can be instigated by the Attorney General. What litigants in personal injury claims often find however is that the Attorney General prefers such referrals to come from the court, which will be best placed to provide an objective assessment as to whether there has been a potential contempt. Failing a referral from the court, the onus is on the litigant to pursue proceedings for contempt of court themselves. The vast majority of contempt proceedings in this area of law are brought by one of the parties, as opposed to the Attorney General.

The law in relation to contempt of court has been developed to enable courts to penalise conduct that can obstruct the administration of justice or be an abuse of the justice system. Should a court find that the respondent is guilty of contempt of court then the court has a range of penalties that can be imposed.

Initial considerations

A party applying to bring proceedings for contempt of court must consider not only whether the incident complained of does amount to a contempt of court, but in addition, does the bringing of such proceedings further the overriding objective. Of particular relevance when considering proceedings for contempt is the following extract of the overriding objective from ***CPR 1.1***:

> *(1)* ***These Rules are a new procedural code with the overriding objective of enabling the court to deal with cases justly and at proportionate cost.***
>
> *(2)* ***Dealing with a case justly and at proportionate cost includes, so far as is practicable –***
>
> ...

> (f) ***enforcing compliance with rules, practice directions and orders.***

There are many forms of contempt, and a detailed discussion of them is beyond the remit of this book. The most common reason for bringing proceedings for contempt of court when it is linked to the issue of surveillance evidence, is because there has been a false statement of truth made, ***CPR 32.14*** provides:

> ***Proceedings for contempt of court may be brought against a person who makes or causes to be made a false statement in a document, prepared in anticipation of or during proceedings and verified by a statement of truth, without an honest belief in its truth.***

The overriding objective emphasises the need for the court to enforce compliance with rules, and a false statement of truth is potentially a breach of ***CPR 32.14***, this is often relied upon to bring proceedings for contempt of court.

When proceedings for contempt of court are being instigated, permission needs to be obtained from the court, pursuant to ***CPR 81.3(5)(b)*** which provides:

> ***(5) Permission to make a contempt application is required where the application is made in relation to—***
>
> ***(b) an allegation of knowingly making a false statement in any affidavit, affirmation or other document verified by a statement of truth or in a disclosure statement.***

The procedural framework for proceedings for contempt of court is found in ***CPR 81***. On 1 October 2020, ***The Civil Procedure (Amendment No 3) Rules 2020 (SI 2020/747)*** introduced significant amendments to CPR 81 and streamlined the rule, in addition Practice Direction 81 was revoked.

Evidential test

When considering if the respondent to contempt proceedings is guilty of a contempt of court, the starting point is set out in the case of ***Carol Walton v Joanne Kirk [2009] EWHC 703 (QB).*** In this case, surveillance evidence had been taken of the claimant which showed her functional capabilities to be greater than the capabilities she had presented in her statements of case. Following conclusion of the claim for damages, proceedings for contempt of court were brought.

The high court held that the respondent to proceedings for contempt is entitled to know precisely the nature of the case that they had to meet. The court reminded parties that discrepancies between a statement of case verified with a statement of truth, and footage seen in video surveillance evidence, does not automatically give rise to a contempt of court. The allegations of contempt must be proved beyond reasonable doubt and any genuine doubt had to be resolved in favour of the respondent. This can give a practical consideration for applicants in contempt proceedings, because claimants may be given the benefit of the doubt because their medical position may fluctuate, and a claimant may therefore be given some latitude by a court.

In ***Walton*** whilst the court found the respondent to be in contempt of court on two counts, the majority of the counts were dismissed. The greater the exaggeration, the less likely it is that the court will believe that the maker of the statement held an honest belief in its truth.

To reinforce the rule that it does not automatically follow that discrepancies in a litigant's case, when compared with surveillance evidence, automatically lead to a finding of contempt of court, the court noted in ***Aviva Insurance Ltd v Kovacic [2017] EWHC 2772 (QB)*** that:

> ***discrepancies between a factual assertion verified by a statement of truth, on the one hand, and video surveillance evidence, on the other, do not automatically give rise to a contempt of court. Ultimately, it is a matter of fact and degree. Some exaggeration may be natural, even understandable.***

This reinforces the position as discussed above in ***Widlake***, a degree of 'white lies' being told in litigation has been accepted by the court of appeal. Just as in fundamental dishonesty, such a position does not automatically lead to a claimant being guilty of a contempt of court.

Penalties

If the respondent to the proceedings has been found guilty of a contempt of court, then the court has a wide discretion when passing sentence as to the penalty that it will impose. Pursuant to ***s14(1) Contempt of Court Act (1981)*** the court can impose an immediate custodial sentence of two years in the case of committal by a superior court, or one month in the case of committal by an inferior court. It should be noted that ***s258(2) Criminal Justice Act (2003)*** sets out that the convicted contemnor is entitled to an unconditional release after serving half of their sentence.

Other powers available to the court include an ability to impose a fine in accordance with ***s14(2) Contempt of Court Act (1981)***, this fine can be unlimited unless it is imposed by an inferior court, in which case it is limited to £2,500. Furthermore, the court can also order the confiscation of assets pursuant to ***CPR 81.9***.

A custodial sentence is not inevitable if the applicant succeeds with the contempt proceedings, the court can suspend a custodial sentence, the sentence imposed will always depend upon the facts of each case. In ***South Wales Fire and Rescue Service v Smith [2011] EWHC 1740 (Admin)***, the high court held that a custodial sentence is likely to be imposed on a party who has made a false disclosure statement. The court will have regard to the following factors when considering the appropriate sentence:

- How prolonged the contempt was;
- How extensive the contempt was;
- The motive for the contempt being committed;
- The extent or risk of harm. Although it must be borne in mind that the court does recognise that there is always harm to the

public interest where false statements have been made to the court.

In addition, further relevant factors were set out in ***Otkritie v International Investment Management Ltd v Gersamia and another [2015] EWHC 821 (Comm),*** which include:

- The court should bear in mind the desirability of keeping offenders, particularly first-time offenders, out of prison;
- Imprisonment is only appropriate where there is "serious, contumacious flouting of orders of the court";
- The key questions are culpability and harm.

It should be noted that ***Otkritie*** is a case originating in the commercial court. In personal injury claims, issues surrounding contempt of court, most commonly arise through false statements of truth rather than breaching court orders as noted above in ***Otkritie***. The decision in ***Otkritie*** is important to consider though as it establishes that the key questions in considering sentence are those of culpability and harm.

In the case of ***George Eliot Hospital NHS Trust v Lesley Maria Elder [2019] EWHC 1813 (QB)***, the high court, an NHS trust applied for the committal of the respondent for contempt of court in light of false statements she had made in her clinical negligence claim brought against the hospital following surgical treatment. The court held:

> ***A five-month custodial term was imposed on a contemnor who had made deliberate and persistent false statements verified by statements of truth in her clinical negligence claim against an NHS trust for the purpose of recovering significant sums of money from a public body. Given the seriousness of the contempt of court, immediate custody was appropriate.***

The court has to consider the following factors in mitigation when handing down its sentence:

- Whether, and if so when, the defendant has admitted the contempt;

- Whether the defendant has expressed remorse;
- Whether the defendant has complied belatedly with the order or otherwise made amends for the wrong;
- The defendant's character and antecedents.

MORE BOOKS BY LAW BRIEF PUBLISHING

A selection of our other titles available now:-

'A Practical Guide to Solicitor and Client Costs – 2nd Edition' by Robin Dunne
'Constructive Dismissal – Practice Pointers and Principles' by Benjimin Burgher
'A Practical Guide to Religion and Belief Discrimination Claims in the Workplace' by Kashif Ali
'A Practical Guide to the Law of Medical Treatment Decisions' by Ben Troke
'Fundamental Dishonesty and QOCS in Personal Injury Proceedings: Law and Practice' by Jake Rowley
'A Practical Guide to the Law in Relation to School Exclusions' by Charlotte Hadfield & Alice de Coverley
'A Practical Guide to Divorce for the Silver Separators' by Karin Walker
'The Right to be Forgotten – The Law and Practical Issues' by Melissa Stock
'A Practical Guide to Planning Law and Rights of Way in National Parks, the Broads and AONBs' by James Maurici QC, James Neill et al
'A Practical Guide to Election Law' by Tom Tabori
'A Practical Guide to the Law in Relation to Surrogacy' by Andrew Powell
'A Practical Guide to Claims Arising from Fatal Accidents – 2nd Edition' by James Patience
'A Practical Guide to the Ownership of Employee Inventions – From Entitlement to Compensation' by James Tumbridge & Ashley Roughton
'A Practical Guide to Asbestos Claims' by Jonathan Owen & Gareth McAloon
'A Practical Guide to Stamp Duty Land Tax in England and Northern Ireland' by Suzanne O'Hara
'A Practical Guide to the Law of Farming Partnerships' by Philip Whitcomb

'Covid-19, Homeworking and the Law – The Essential Guide to Employment and GDPR Issues' by Forbes Solicitors
'Covid-19, Force Majeure and Frustration of Contracts – The Essential Guide' by Keith Markham
'Covid-19 and Criminal Law – The Essential Guide' by Ramya Nagesh
'Covid-19 and Family Law in England and Wales – The Essential Guide' by Safda Mahmood
'A Practical Guide to the Law of Unlawful Eviction and Harassment – 2nd Edition' by Stephanie Lovegrove
'Covid-19, Residential Property, Equity Release and Enfranchisement – The Essential Guide' by Paul Sams and Louise Uphill
'Covid-19, Brexit and the Law of Commercial Leases – The Essential Guide' by Mark Shelton
'A Practical Guide to Costs in Personal Injury Claims – 2nd Edition' by Matthew Hoe
'A Practical Guide to the General Data Protection Regulation (GDPR) – 2nd Edition' by Keith Markham
'Ellis on Credit Hire – Sixth Edition' by Aidan Ellis & Tim Kevan
'A Practical Guide to Working with Litigants in Person and McKenzie Friends in Family Cases' by Stuart Barlow
'Protecting Unregistered Brands: A Practical Guide to the Law of Passing Off' by Lorna Brazell
'A Practical Guide to Secondary Liability and Joint Enterprise Post-Jogee' by Joanne Cecil & James Mehigan
'A Practical Guide to the Pre-Action RTA Claims Protocol for Personal Injury Lawyers' by Antonia Ford
'A Practical Guide to Neighbour Disputes and the Law' by Alexander Walsh
'A Practical Guide to Forfeiture of Leases' by Mark Shelton
'A Practical Guide to Coercive Control for Legal Practitioners and Victims' by Rachel Horman

'A Practical Guide to Rights Over Airspace and Subsoil' by Daniel Gatty
'Tackling Disclosure in the Criminal Courts – A Practitioner's Guide' by Narita Bahra QC & Don Ramble
'A Practical Guide to the Law of Driverless Cars – Second Edition' by Alex Glassbrook, Emma Northey & Scarlett Milligan
'A Practical Guide to TOLATA Claims' by Greg Williams
'Artificial Intelligence – The Practical Legal Issues' by John Buyers
'A Practical Guide to the Law of Prescription in Scotland' by Andrew Foyle
'A Practical Guide to the Construction and Rectification of Wills and Trust Instruments' by Edward Hewitt
'A Practical Guide to the Law of Bullying and Harassment in the Workplace' by Philip Hyland
'How to Be a Freelance Solicitor: A Practical Guide to the SRA-Regulated Freelance Solicitor Model' by Paul Bennett
'A Practical Guide to Prison Injury Claims' by Malcolm Johnson
'A Practical Guide to the Small Claims Track' by Dominic Bright
'A Practical Guide to Advising Clients at the Police Station' by Colin Stephen McKeown-Beaumont
'A Practical Guide to Antisocial Behaviour Injunctions' by Iain Wightwick
'Practical Mediation: A Guide for Mediators, Advocates, Advisers, Lawyers, and Students in Civil, Commercial, Business, Property, Workplace, and Employment Cases' by Jonathan Dingle with John Sephton
'The Mini-Pupillage Workbook' by David Boyle
'A Practical Guide to Crofting Law' by Brian Inkster
'A Practical Guide to Spousal Maintenance' by Liz Cowell
'A Practical Guide to the Law of Domain Names and Cybersquatting' by Andrew Clemson
'A Practical Guide to the Law of Gender Pay Gap Reporting' by Harini Iyengar

'A Practical Guide to the Rights of Grandparents in Children Proceedings' by Stuart Barlow
'NHS Whistleblowing and the Law' by Joseph England
'Employment Law and the Gig Economy' by Nigel Mackay & Annie Powell
'A Practical Guide to Noise Induced Hearing Loss (NIHL) Claims' by Andrew Mckie, Ian Skeate, Gareth McAloon
'An Introduction to Beauty Negligence Claims – A Practical Guide for the Personal Injury Practitioner' by Greg Almond
'Intercompany Agreements for Transfer Pricing Compliance' by Paul Sutton
'Zen and the Art of Mediation' by Martin Plowman
'A Practical Guide to the SRA Principles, Individual and Law Firm Codes of Conduct 2019 – What Every Law Firm Needs to Know' by Paul Bennett
'A Practical Guide to Adoption for Family Lawyers' by Graham Pegg
'A Practical Guide to Industrial Disease Claims' by Andrew Mckie & Ian Skeate
'A Practical Guide to Redundancy' by Philip Hyland
'A Practical Guide to Vicarious Liability' by Mariel Irvine
'A Practical Guide to Applications for Landlord's Consent and Variation of Leases' by Mark Shelton
'A Practical Guide to Relief from Sanctions Post-Mitchell and Denton' by Peter Causton
'A Practical Guide to Equity Release for Advisors' by Paul Sams
'A Practical Guide to the Law Relating to Food' by Ian Thomas
'A Practical Guide to Financial Services Claims' by Chris Hegarty
'The Law of Houses in Multiple Occupation: A Practical Guide to HMO Proceedings' by Julian Hunt
'A Practical Guide to Unlawful Eviction and Harassment' by Stephanie Lovegrove
'Occupiers, Highways and Defective Premises Claims: A Practical Guide Post-Jackson – 2nd Edition' by Andrew Mckie

'A Practical Guide to Financial Ombudsman Service Claims' by Adam Temple & Robert Scrivenor
'A Practical Guide to Advising Schools on Employment Law' by Jonathan Holden
'A Practical Guide to Running Housing Disrepair and Cavity Wall Claims: 2nd Edition' by Andrew Mckie & Ian Skeate
'A Practical Guide to Holiday Sickness Claims – 2nd Edition' by Andrew Mckie & Ian Skeate
'Arguments and Tactics for Personal Injury and Clinical Negligence Claims' by Dorian Williams
'A Practical Guide to Drone Law' by Rufus Ballaster, Andrew Firman, Eleanor Clot
'A Practical Guide to Compliance for Personal Injury Firms Working With Claims Management Companies' by Paul Bennett
'A Practical Guide to Dog Law for Owners and Others' by Andrea Pitt
'RTA Allegations of Fraud in a Post-Jackson Era: The Handbook – 2nd Edition' by Andrew Mckie
'RTA Personal Injury Claims: A Practical Guide Post-Jackson' by Andrew Mckie
'On Experts: CPR35 for Lawyers and Experts' by David Boyle
'An Introduction to Personal Injury Law' by David Boyle
'A Practical Guide to Subtle Brain Injury Claims' by Pankaj Madan

These books and more are available to order online direct from the publisher at www.lawbriefpublishing.com, where you can also read free sample chapters. For any queries, contact us on 0844 587 2383 or mail@lawbriefpublishing.com.

Our books are also usually in stock at www.amazon.co.uk with free next day delivery for Prime members, and at good legal bookshops such as Wildy & Sons.

We are regularly launching new books in our series of practical day-to-day practitioners' guides. Visit our website and join our free newsletter to be kept informed and to receive special offers, free chapters, etc.

You can also follow us on Twitter at www.twitter.com/lawbriefpub.

www.ingramcontent.com/pod-product-compliance
Ingram Content Group UK Ltd.
Pitfield, Milton Keynes, MK11 3LW, UK
UKHW020148290926
15471UKWH00004B/760

9 781913 715731